Chick **TV**

Television and Popular Culture
Robert J. Thompson, *Series Editor*

Select Titles in Television and Popular Culture

Becoming: Genre, Queerness, and Transformation in NBC's "Hannibal"
    Kavita Mudan Finn and EJ Nielsen, eds.

*Black Male Frames: African Americans in a Century
of Hollywood Cinema, 1903–2003*
    Roland Leander Williams Jr.

*Captain America, Masculinity, and Violence:
The Evolution of a National Icon*
    J. Richard Stevens

*Gladiators in Suits: Race, Gender, and the Politics
of Representation in "Scandal"*
    Simone Adams, Kimberly R. Moffitt, and Ronald L. Jackson II, eds.

Perspectives on "Crazy Ex-Girlfriend": Nuanced Postnetwork Television
    Amanda Konkle and Charles Burnetts, eds.

Screwball Television: Critical Perspectives on "Gilmore Girls"
    David Scott Diffrient and David Lavery, eds.

Television Finales: From "Howdy Doody" to "Girls"
    Douglas L. Howard and David Bianculli, eds.

Watching TV with a Linguist
    Kristy Beers Fägersten, ed.

For a full list of titles in this series,
visit https://press.syr.edu/supressbook-series
/television-and-popular-culture/.

Chick TV

Antiheroines and Time Unbound

Yael Levy

Syracuse University Press

Copyright © 2022 by Syracuse University Press

Syracuse, New York 13244-5290

All Rights Reserved

First Edition 2022

22 23 24 25 26 27   6 5 4 3 2 1

∞ The paper used in this publication meets the minimum requirements of the American National Standard for Information Sciences—Permanence of Paper for Printed Library Materials, ANSI Z39.48-1992.

For a listing of books published and distributed by Syracuse University Press, visit https://press.syr.edu.

ISBN: 978-0-8156-3738-7 (hardcover)
      978-0-8156-3724-0 (paperback)
      978-0-8156-5525-1 (e-book)

Library of Congress Cataloging-in-Publication Data
Names: Levy, Yael (College teacher) author.
Title: Chick TV: antiheroines and time unbound / Yael Levy.
Description: First edition. | Syracuse : Syracuse University Press, 2022. | Series: Television and popular culture | Includes bibliographical references and index. | Summary: "Drawing on the potential of both temporality and antiheroinism to invoke feminist resistance, this research suggests a correlation between televisual temporality and antiheroinism in early 2000s US television drama series, examines that correlation, and explores the feminist politics of these two narrative apparatuses"— Provided by publisher.
Identifiers: LCCN 2021025484 (print) | LCCN 2021025485 (ebook) | ISBN 9780815637387 (hardcover) | ISBN 9780815637240 (paperback) | ISBN 9780815655251 (ebook)
Subjects: LCSH: Television series—United States—History and criticism. | Antiheroes on television. | Space and time on television. | Television and politics—United States. | Feminism.
Classification: LCC PN1992.8.S4 L489 2022 (print) | LCC PN1992.8.S4 (ebook) | DDC 791.450973—dc23
LC record available at https://lccn.loc.gov/2021025484
LC ebook record available at https://lccn.loc.gov/2021025485

Manufactured in the United States of America

Contents

Acknowledgments   *vii*

Introduction: *The Complexities of Chick TV*   *1*
1. Resistance   *31*
2. Deviation   *50*
3. Serialization   *79*
4. Rewriting   *107*
   Conclusion: *Reclaiming "Chick" for TV*   *143*

Appendix: *Antiheroines Positioned along the Continua*   *153*
References   *157*
Index   *175*

Acknowledgments

My gratitude is first indebted to the feminist scholars who paved the way to profound research of women's culture, inspired by all things "chick," and to the women characters of chick TV who were my own inspiration. To my teachers and colleagues at Tel Aviv University, I am primarily grateful to Anat Zanger and her invaluable insights throughout this project and to Raz Yosef and Boaz Hagin for always constructive advice. I thank Lynne Joyrich and Orly Lubin for their wise thoughts on previous versions of this book; Robert Thompson, Deborah Manion, and the board and staff at Syracuse University Press for creative cooperation; and anonymous readers throughout the process for being so generous with their time and input. To Lynn Spigel, Victoria Johnson, Jennifer Mclearen, Diane Negra, and Linda Dittmar, thank you for advice, feedback, and challenging conversation. Finally, I am truly grateful for the enduring support of the Tisch School of Film and Television and the Arts Faculty at Tel Aviv University.

Parts of chapter 1 were published in "Girls' Issues: The Feminist Politics of Girls' Celebration of the 'Trivial,'" in *Girls and the Awkward Politics of Gender, Race, and Privilege*, edited by Elwood Watson, Jennifer Mitchell, Marc E. Shaw (Lanham: Lexington Books, 2015), 63–70 (all rights reserved and reprinted with permission). The chapter is reprinted with permission by Rowman and Littlefield (all rights reserved). An early version of chapter 3 was published as "Serial Housewives: The Feminist Resistance of *The Real Housewives*' Matrixial Structure," *Continuum: Journal of Media and Cultural Studies* 32, no. 3 (2018), 370–80, DOI: 10.1080/10304312.2018.1450492. Reprinted by permission of Taylor & Francis, https://www.tandfonline.com.

Chick **TV**

Introduction

The Complexities of Chick TV

The formidable, charming moral relativist Tony Soprano is often considered to have ushered in the era of the television antihero. Being an identifiable protagonist who lacks certain heroic qualities—such as sacrificing himself for the greater good or, in general, working to promote good—marked him as a complex, multilayered character worthy of popular interest and academic analysis. The narrative that surrounded him was also perceived as complex, as it amalgamated various forms of storytelling devices and aesthetic features, most specifically such that play with plot linearity in favor of flashbacks, surreal dream sequences, and other modes of temporal play. Correspondingly, discourse around television, both academic and popular, has recognized that the twenty-first century has seen the rise of the televisual antihero (Poniewozik and Winters 2007; Murray 2008; Christian 2010; Martin 2013; Mittell 2015a; Bruun Vaage 2016; Menon 2008; Bradshaw 2013; Tally 2016; Buonanno 2017; Petridis 2017; Haas, Pierce, and Busl 2020; Brost 2020) as well as of temporal narrative complexity (Ames 2012; Mittell 2006; Booth 2012; Kelly 2017; Shimpach 2010). Interestingly, both of these features of complexity—characterization and temporality—have been examined chiefly via men's characters, most notably Tony Soprano (*The Sopranos*, 1999–2007) and the continuing lineage of Don Draper (*Mad Men*, 2007–15), Walter White (*Breaking Bad*, 2008–13), Dexter Morgan (*Dexter*, 2006–13), and other (usually white, heterosexual) men, and the perceivably masculine genres they inhabit, from crime dramas to suspense thrillers.

This era of antiheroes and complex narratives generated ubiquitous recognition of a surge of televisual sophistication but seems to have left out the place of women. Complex antiheroines were often dismissed as marginal or just not antiheroic enough (they may be "prickly" but too "sympathetic" or "comedic," Mittell notes in his seminal *Complex TV*), and complex narrative was a label reserved for genres that tend "toward masculine appeals" (Mittell 2015a, 150). This book sets out to explore the complexities of "chick TV"—television about and addressed to women, with a focus on dialogue and relationships, women's issues and desires, in the tradition of "chick lit" and "chick flicks"—specifically in regard to its complex characterization of antiheroines and complex temporality. Multilayered complexity, I contend, is present not only in the morally questionable cop or lawyer that is inhabiting stereotypically masculine genres such as action or procedurals but also in the housewife or nurse who inhabits more stereotypically feminine texts, such as family dramas, romance dramedies, or docusoaps, and whose trivialized flaws are in fact a form of antiheroic feminist resistance.

Drawing on the potential of both temporality and antiheroinism to invoke feminist resistance to hegemonic ideologies by representing marginalized women's stories, celebrating trivialized women's issues, and gaining women's agency, this book outlines the ways in which various forms of textual temporalities—intradiegetic temporality; temporal constructs such as flashback and flashforward and their position in episodes; temporal structures in the layout of series and the temporality of seriality; the temporality of intertextuality—are linked to the characterization of 2000s' television antiheroines in the United States.

Chick TV: Women's Genres in US Television

The terms "chick lit" and "chick flick" refer to literature and films that feature women's stories and target women audiences (Ferriss and Young 2006 and 2008). Following in the tradition of "chick" texts, television that focuses on women characters and their stories corresponds with "women's genres" (soapy, melodramatic, stylized), articulated by Annette Kuhn as the "construction of narratives motivated by female desire and processes of spectator identification governed by female point-of-view" (1984, 18). More specific to the televisual context, the chick TV texts of the twenty-first century are often rooted in the tradition of soap operas in terms of their focus on dialogue rather than action, relationships rather than adventures, family and the domestic space rather than the public space, emotional struggles rather than professional ones, and women's concerns and desires rather than men's (Fiske 1987; Hatch 2002).

Of course, the distinction of women's culture is as constructed as gender itself, and "chick TV" is consequently a discursive concept resulting from conservative and economic interests served by essentializing for the purpose of consumption and marketability. Chick TV series do not inherently have greater ties to women; this tie is the result of popular and critical discourse that perpetuates gendered categories. Nevertheless, since the cultural construction of women's texts exists in the world, with executives, producers, advertisers, consumers, critics, and viewers perceiving television through gendered classification, this book seeks to examine this arguably overlooked category rather than question its boundaries to reveal its radical potential despite perceived inferiority.

Part of the constructedness of the term "chick" is that it is often used pejoratively to establish feminine culture as déclassé and designed to entertain and not be thought-provoking. Given this line of thinking, even acclaimed televisual texts that contain chick aspects (dominance of women characters, women's issues, family and relationships, dialogue and emotion) may be subject to devaluation. Approaching the "soapy," a term quite typically delivered with disdain, is associated with low production values, farfetched plots, and stretched narratives. But the disdain attached to the term is also directed at texts inclined toward what is regarded as feminine (Blumenthal 1997; Brunsdon 2000; Nussbaum 2018). Chick TV is thus a label attached to television that revolves around the experiences of women, specifically experiences that are often trivialized in culture, such as those that involve relationships, friendships, the body, fashion, and women's sexual desire.[1]

Disregard of women's culture as an art form has remained a traditional constant since medieval chivalric romances of courtly love (Harzewski 2006), to women's literature (Woolf 2000 [1929]), and on to contemporary women's culture (Brunsdon 2000). According to Lynn Spigel, artifacts of chick culture have also been repudiated by feminists (Spigel 2004), who perceived their pop inclination as "apolitical" (Grdešić 2013, 357). The cultural dismissal of chick culture has produced a belated academic perception of the profundities of art that is associated with women, such as melodramas (Kaplan 1983; Modleski 2002; Byars 1991; and Williams 1998) and soap operas (Lopate 1977; Modleski 1979; Mattelart 1981; and Hobson 1982). As its cultural predecessors, from the woman's novel to soap operas, chick TV's insistence on celebrating that which is culturally marginalized due to its association with the feminine is in itself political.

While many twenty-first-century television series inform this book's analyses, a closer examination is devoted to eight series. Each of the four chapters is dedicated to a different layer of the feminist politics of the antiheroine-temporality correlation in chick TV. Each chapter focuses on a main case study that best serves the chapter's interpretive perspective, with comparative analyses in the background. The first chapter, "Resistance," examines key hypotheses via the high production value, women's-culture oriented, single-protagonist led *Girls* (2012–17).[2] Chapter 2, "Deviation," does so via the soap-operatic medical drama *Grey's Anatomy* (2005–), which features various women characters of different ages, sexualities, and races. Chapter 3, "Serialization," examines the highly aspirational docusoap franchise *The Real Housewives* (2006–), while the fourth chapter, "Rewriting,"

---

1. Kyra Hunting analyzes *Sex and the City*, *Lipstick Jungle*, and *The Cashmere Mafia* as "chick-lit television," which she defines as "a cultural category that responds to the evolving gender norms in American culture" (2012, 188).

2. Though *Girls* is an ensemble show, much of the narrative is focalized through the eyes of the more dominant main character Hannah Horvath.

uses the soap-operatic ensemble mystery dramedy *Desperate Housewives* (2004–12). Throughout the chapters, comparative analyses are devoted to the single-protagonist led dramedy *Nurse Jackie* (2009–15), the single-protagonist led drama *Being Mary Jane* (2013–19), the high production value family drama *Six Feet Under* (2001–5), and the ensemble docusoap *Sister Wives* (2010–). Though not an exhaustive list of early twenty-first-century chick TV, these texts were selected for their compatibility with the theoretical framework. All are chick TV insofar as they are rooted in or are evocative of the tradition of women's genres, specifically soap operas in the televisual context, in their focus on dialogue, relationships, family, intimacy, emotional struggles, women's lives, issues, and desires (Hatch 2002).

The bounds of chick TV and the cultural framework on which they are based are constructed and meandering, and whether a particular text meets the criteria remains debatable. Arguably, other examples may be categorized as chick TV, such as *Jane the Virgin* (2014–19), *Transparent* (2014–19), *Crazy Ex-Girlfriend* (2015–19), to name a few. However, each of the study cases was chosen because it best exemplifies specific features of chick TV antiheroines and temporality. Conversely, texts based on "men's genres"—such as the police procedural *The Closer* (2005–12), the legal thriller *Damages* (2007–12), the crime drama *Saving Grace* (2007–10), the legal procedural *The Good Wife* (2009–16), the political thriller *Homeland* (2011–20), the political suspense drama *Scandal* (2012–18), the science fiction action drama *Orphan Black* (2013–17), the prison drama *Orange Is the New Black* (2013–19), the murder mystery *How to Get Away with Murder* (2014–20), the science fiction western *Westworld* (2016–), the dystopian drama *The Handmaid's Tale* (2017–), the spy thriller *Killing Eve* (2018–), or the psychological thriller *Sharp Objects* (2018)—are not analyzed in depth despite their presentation of women as main characters, with some distinctly exhibiting antiheroine characteristics.[3] In

---

3. I would argue that the dominant presence of women characters often shapes the cultural and industrial categorization of a text more than its other qualities do, including genre affiliations and production values. This point is demonstrated, for

the same vein, I will not address women-led sitcoms, game shows, variety shows, and other subgenres that are not traditionally gendered as "feminine." Chick TV framing thus includes family dramas, comic dramas that lean toward the emotional, romantic dramas, docusoaps, and other generic constructions that foreground women's stories.[4]

Within chick TV's generic coordinates, the classification may apply to diverse stylization and branding variations and inevitably overlap with other televisual classifications, some of which seem conflicting. For example, though the premise of this book leans on the marginalization of series that feature women's issues and women characters, it bears noting that not all chick TV texts are denigrated or perceived as "pulp" television. *Six Feet Under*, for instance, has been outwardly addressed as complex television (Mittell 2015a; McCabe and Akass 2007) despite its chick TV dominance of women characters and focus on family and dialogue. Relatedly, though the medical drama was predominantly male-centered in its early days, the genre has gradually obtained more "soapy" elements in its later incarnations (Jacobs 2003), of which the melodramatic *Grey's Anatomy* is a principal case in point. Correspondingly, the docusoap—the reality subset driven mostly by the stories of cast members (Murray and Ouellette 2009), focusing on family and relationships, and combining "observational documentary techniques with serial narrative techniques of soap opera" (Hill 2005, 23)—forms a reality version of chick TV. More often than not, a chick TV text would be both compatible with the subgenre's qualities and with other televisual categories. By examining different forms of chick TV series, I delineate the feminist work

---

example, in John Fiske's discussion of the genre hybridity of *Cagney & Lacey* and the eventual generic labeling of the show "away from masculine cop show towards soap opera or woman's show" due to its higher ratings when scheduled with other "women's" shows (1987, 112).

4. For more elaborate analyses of non-chick-TV antiheroines in twenty-first-century US television, see Tally (2016); Buonanno (2017); Haas, Pierce, and Busl (2020); Brost (2020); and Pinedo (2021).

of the core features of chick TV, most specifically in relation to temporality and antiheroines.

A Rebel of Many Causes: Antiheroes and Antiheroines

Drawing from Murray Smith (1995), Jason Mittell (2015a) states that "an antihero is a character who is our primary point of ongoing narrative alignment but whose behavior and beliefs provoke ambiguous, conflicted, or negative moral allegiance" (142–43). According to Neil Cartridge, that antiheroes "fail to live up to the very definition of heroism suggested by the texts in which they appear" (2012, 3) calls into question ideological conventions, thus working, as articulated by Victor Brombert, to "challenge the relevance of handed-down assumptions, induce the reader to reexamine moral categories, and deal, often disturbingly, with the survival of values" (1999, 6). The character of the antihero thus serves to call social norms into question and shed light on that which is constituted as heroic by working to "deflate, subvert, and challenge an 'ideal' image" (5).

Antiheroic characterization can be detected throughout American television history, from *Maverick*'s Bret Maverick (1957–62), who toyed with the notion of moral indiscretions (though mostly opting for the moral high road) to *Murphy Brown*'s Murphy Brown (1988–98), who consciously resisted the demands placed on women (including one famous extradiegetic dispute with Dan Quayle about single mothers), with characters that protest and disrupt the social order.[5] However, many critics have insisted that the representation of *The Sopranos*' (1999–2007) Tony Soprano has marked a shift in the history of television antiheroes and perhaps in the history of antiheroes

5. Percy Adams (1976) argues that the antihero has been ever-present in literature since nearly all heroes possess antiheroic traits, starting with the early examples of David, Gilgamesh, and Odysseus. Similarly, the antihero can be found along the history of cinematic representations as a "symbol of social protest, emotional distress and family disruption" (Garbarz 2013).

in general. According to James Keegan Poniewozik and Rebecca Winters,

> You could organize the history of TV dramas into B.T. and A.T.: Before Tony and After Tony. Before *The Sopranos*, TV drama was mainly divided between good guys and bad guys (with the odd exception like NYPD Blue's Andy Sipowicz). Tony Soprano and his followers on HBO, FX and elsewhere showed that audiences would follow villains with sympathetic qualities and heroes with addictive, self-destructive personalities. Move over, good guys and bad guys, these dramas said. Make room for the good-bad guy. (2007, 57)

This perception of television antiheroism as apotheosized at the turn of the twenty-first century is a common one in both popular discourse and scholarly writing (Murray 2008; Christian 2010; Martin 2013; Mittell 2015a; Bruun Vaage 2016).

A significant feature of this twenty-first century apotheosized antiheroism, directly addressed by some scholars and social commentators and unmentioned as an unsurprising obviousness by others, is the fact that it has only been observed and analyzed with regard to male characters. Poniewozik and Winters note in reference to the 2000s epitomizing of the "good-bad guy" in television that "the operative word . . . was guy . . . The shows focused on male antiheroes and their loud, angsty Y-chromosome dramas: Tony, *The Shield*'s Vic Mackey, *Rescue Me*'s Tommy Gavin, *Dexter*'s serial killer Dexter Morgan, *Deadwood*'s Al Swearengen, *24*'s Jack Bauer" (Poniewozik and Winters 2007, 57. Women's antiheroics were not perceived to have been explored by televisual texts in the third millennium. According to Mittell, there was a surge of antiheroes and a lack of antiheroines, because "men are more likely to be respected and admired for ruthlessness, self-promotion, and the pursuit of success at any cost, while women are still constructed more as nurturing, selfless, and objects of action rather than empowered agents themselves" (2015a, 150). Even when "allowed lives beyond merely being either obstacles or facilitators to the male hero's progress . . . free to be venal, ruthless, misguided," women characters were "most often relegated to supporting roles" (Martin 2013, 5), such as *The Sopranos*' Carmela (1999–2007) or *Mad Men*'s Peggy (2007–15), or *Breaking Bad*'s Skyler (2008–13).[6] Women characters "did not . . . qualify for membership in the antihero clubhouse" (Menon 2008).

Adriana Clavel-Vazquez adds that more often than not, women who exhibit antiheroinist qualities are labeled as villainesses rather than as antiheroines, stemming from a "resistance to morally transgressive female characters" (2018, 206).[7] Perhaps antiheroines are ubiquitous, Clavel-Vazquez's observation suggests, but they are not labeled as such. Perhaps instead of being perceived as complex, multilayered antiheroines, as are their male counterparts, twenty-first-century antiheroines have been "dismissed as bitches, psychos or bunny boilers" (Pilger, quoted in Hughes 2014). Milly Buonanno addresses this inconspicuous sexism as well, as she protests the "narrow understanding of the antihero complex nature, along with the hegemonic pretension that masculine templates should mould female characters, and implied inattention and dismissal for worthy antiheroines that did not measure up to the antiheroic standard of Tony Soprano or Walter White, or Don Draper for that matter" (2017, 8). The third millennium did not fail to introduce antiheroic women. Rather, it used "masculine templates" to judge antiheroes, thereby disqualifying women characters from the label of antiheroine. Buonanno ties the dismissal of antiheroine characters as villainesses—versus the adoration of complex men characters as antiheroes—to the destabilization of gender norms

---

6. Margrethe Bruun Vaage similarly notes that while antiheroes were culturally lauded for their characterizational complexities, women characters who serve as antiheroes' wives were often hated by viewers (2016, 151).

7. As Sundi Rose-Holt put it, "male characters who are flawed and multidimensional (often with horrible acts of their own doing in their past) are called antiheroes, but women are called villains" (2015). Relatedly, though Mittell argues there is "a distinct lack" of antiheroics manifested in women, he notes that such a character would likely be "viewed as more of an unsympathetic 'ball-busting bitch' than the charismatic rogue that typifies most male antiheroes" (2015a, 150).

that valuing women's moral or social transgression might engender. She notes that regarding women as antiheroines might disrupt the social order because women are expected to maintain order. "Female transgressive agency," Buonanno asserts, "does not just break social norms but violates and subverts the natural properties of true womanhood" (2017, 11).

It seems, then, that in order to reveal the antiheroic mode in women characters, a different hermeneutic strategy is needed, as women's antiheroics (that is, antiheroinism) is manifested differently from that of men. Significantly, late 2010s scholarship introduced a newly articulated set of interpretive approaches that focus on antiheroinism as different from, rather than derivative of, antiheroism. These approaches explored antiheroinism's association with unlikability (Brost 2020), its ties to motherhood and mental illness (Tally 2016; Haas, Pierce, and Busl 2020; Pinedo 2021), or its formulation of "antiaspirationalism" (Silverman and Hagelin 2018) and "trainwreck feminism" (Tully 2020). Though not all the antiheroines in this book align with the gendered idiosyncrasies identified in these researches, what such observations significantly indicate is that there exists a need to look at antiheroinism differently from antiheroism.

Indeed, according to Cartridge, "it is perhaps a distinctively masculine set of failings that tends to shape the construction of antiheroism," and "'antiheroinism' is . . . an essentially different phenomenon." If antiheroism stems from men's failure to adhere to the socially assigned roles of masculinity as moral and assertive authoritarians (Connell 1995) and leaders (Gray and Ginsberg 2007), then antiheroinism stems from women's failure to adhere to their socially assigned roles as nurturers (Connell 1995)—sexual, spiritual, culinarily, or otherwise. What antiheroinism thus shares with antiheroism is that both "challenge the relevance of handed-down assumptions" (Brombert 1999, 6) but, more so than that, both antiheroism and antiheroinism pose challenges to gender assumptions. Consequently, both sets of failings are gendered.

However, seeing as the demands of femininity are different from the demands of masculinity, antiheroinist resistance is different from antiheroic resistance. If antiheroism can be seen to focus on "loud, angsty Y-chromosome dramas" (Poniewozik and Winters 2007, 57), then antiheroinism may focus on "women's worst anxieties about the things that they might do or the ways that they might act—needy, self-centered, sort of melodramatic" (Nussbaum, in Rosenberg and Nussbaum 2013)—and other forms of conduct that might defy the expectation that women "maintain, arrange, and perpetuate this sociosymbolic contract as mothers, wives, nurses, doctors, teachers" (Kristeva 1981, 23–24). Mittell (2015b) notes, for example, that though the character of Rachel of *UnREAL* was modeled after *Breaking Bad*'s Walter White, "her power and persona is quite different than the typical male anti-hero." Rachel, Mittell observes, manipulates "via empathy, . . . by creating an emotional bond," whereas men antiheroes would use "bullying and belittling." In response to Mittell, Battles (in Mittell 2015b) proclaims that the fact that "men and women . . . operate under different sets of conditions" affects the design of antiheroics, as antiheroinism would consider "the ways that patriarchy shapes the lives of women." Thus, inasmuch as women endure social forces that are different from those endured by men (the subtle and not so subtle forms of gendered interactions), so do antiheroines face different social forces from antiheroes, thereby resisting different forces in a different manner.

If "the hero's journey often seeks to bring order to disorder" (Shadraconis 2013, 2), and the antihero's journey is associated with introducing moral disorder to the social order (Mittell 2015a; Brombert 1999), then the antiheroine seeks to bring not only moral disorder—in fact, sometimes it is not about moral disorder at all—but also gender disorder to the hegemonic and patriarchal social order. Moreover, I posit that though both antiheroism and antiheroinism challenge the social order, antiheroism ultimately maintains it, whereas antiheroinism resists it, deviates from it, and envisions an alternative order.

Antiheroinism, gendered as it is, is defined by its distance from hegemony—the antiheroine is a woman character who resists, challenges, or inverts social expectations regarding feminine performance. Seeing as feminine performance is elusive and arbitrary (Butler 1988),

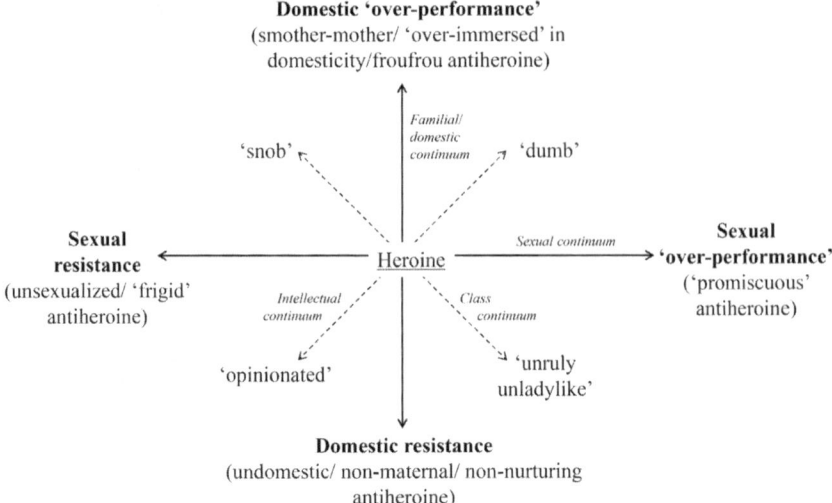

Graph 1. The Antiheroinist Continua

the antiheroine would be the one who "fails" at the level of performance—either not feminine enough (selfish rather than caring, for example) or "too feminine" (smothering rather than caring, for example). Consequently, I propose taxonomizing chick TV antiheroines along two main continua—the domestic continuum and the sexual continuum—and two secondary continua (as they are not directly related to femininity)—the intellectual continuum and the class continuum (graph 1). On each of these continua, the antiheroine can be either "too much" or "too little"—if she were "just right," she would be a heroine—as can be seen in the following diagram.

Typologizing antiheroinism should thus be mapped out in accordance with the type of resistance to patriarchal order that women characters pose, that is, either in refusing to serve as sexual object or in refusing to serve as nurturer/mother.[8] The sexual continuum and

---

8. In *The Queer Art of Failure*, J. Halberstam postulates both nonproduction and nonreproduction as counterhegemonic. "Heteronormative common sense leads to the equation of success with advancement, capital accumulation, family, ethical conduct, and hope. Other subordinate, queer, or counterhegemonic modes of

the familial/domestic continuum roughly overlap with the Madonna/whore dichotomy, by which women are usually characterized either as oversexualized or as desexualized and maternal (a predominant representational mode in western culture, as noted by Myra Macdonald 1995; Naomi Wolf 1998; and Jennifer Musial 2014).[9] In order to perform femininity as demanded by the "sociosymbolic contract" (Kristeva 1981, 23), a woman must be nurturing and mothering on the domestic continuum—maternal, family-oriented, caring for others (Haas, Pierce, and Busl 2020)—and serve as an object of desire without being "too" sexual—accurately fulfilling the "beauty myth" (Naomi Wolf 1991), looked-at without looking (Mulvey 1999 [1975]).

As this book's analyses show, mis-performing femininity is manifested either in failing the domestic ideal (not wanting children or a family, being selfish and uncaring) or in overdoing it (being overimmersed in family and domesticity—"smother-mother," "bridezilla," "froufrou").[10] Likewise it is manifested in either failing the sexual ideal (resisting beauty regimes in appearance, refusing to be looked at, or refusing to engage sexually) or overdoing it (a sexual subject, not object, expressing desire that collides with Laura Mulvey's famous

---

common-sense lead to the association of failure with nonconformity, anticapitalist practices, nonreproductive life styles, negativity, and critique" (2011, 89).

9. Drawing from Margaret Tally (2016), who frames antiheroinism as often resulting from "failed" performances of motherhood, Melanie Haas, N. A. Pierce, and Gretchen Busl address the representation of either of the extremes of the Madonna/whore dichotomy as emphasizing "women as beings without agency or purpose, except as defined by men, and limited to inhabiting accepted social roles." They stress that "the ascent of the antiheroine in contemporary culture challenges the boundaries that limit women to idealized motherhood and domestic partnership, allowing space for narratives that diverge from social prescriptions and characters who embody visions of womanhood that affirm choice, agency, and alterity" (2020, ix).

10. The domestic continuum is tightly correlated with an emotional quality, as the domestic woman is "rightly" emotional, the woman who is "not domestic enough" is perceived as cold, unaffectionate, and noncaring, and the woman who is "too domestic" is perceived as smothering, obsessive, overemotional, or hysteric.

"to-be-looked-at-ness" [1975], labeled "oversexed," "promiscuous," "slut").[11] That both women who resist social scripts and women who "overact" these scripts deviate from what is considered proper emphasizes the arbitrariness of gender performance, thereby rendering both extremes as antiheroinist as both characterizations resist order.[12]

In order to sustain this form of social judgment, by which there is a very limited range of conduct a woman can perform to gain social approval, two other continua work to police the first two, and thus ensure that the validity of each is maintained. The third continuum is the intellectual continuum, by which the proper woman would be wise in matters of family, beauty, and home, but not intellectually perceptive or savvy. If she is either too "dumb" and superficial or too "opinionated" and conceited, she bears the potential to step out of her assigned role as a nurturing object of desire and therefore poses a threat to order (Halberstam 2011; Inness 2007).[13] The fourth continuum is the class continuum, by which the proper woman would be decorous and demure but not haughty or detached. If she is either too "vulgar" and uncouth or too snobbish and pretentious, she may depart from the ladylike behavior expected of her, of "calmness, ease,

---

11. "For teenage girls in particular, the term 'slut' props up a sexual double standard, marks female sexuality as deviant, and works to control girls' behaviour and social positioning" (Attwood 2007, 235).

12. "It is precisely because she embodies the potentiality of turning constructed notions of femininity upside down by eluding or defying gender norms about how women should behave, that the antiheroine character calls for feminist attention and consideration" (Buonanno 2017, 11).

13. Halberstam notes that "stupidity is as profoundly gendered as knowledge formations in general; thus while unknowing in a man is sometimes rendered as part of masculine charm, unknowing in a woman indicates a lack and a justification of a social order that anyway privileges men" (2011, 55). Conversely, Inness (2007) relates to intelligent women characters such as *The Simpsons*' Lisa, *Daria*'s Daria, or *Buffy the Vampire Slayer*'s Willow as "outsiders" and "aberrations" (4–5), noting that "according to the common cultural stereotype, women are not supposed to be too smart and, in particular, are not supposed to be as intelligent as their husbands or boyfriends" (2).

restraint and luxurious decoration" (Allan 2009, 146) and destabilize order.

Though the intellectual continuum and the class continuum are not directly related to women's gender roles, they work to regulate them, as straying from the desired range of intelligence or decorum is often socially penalized as is straying from the desired range of domesticity and sexuality. The continua are thus intertwined, as, for example, women who resist order on either the domestic/familial continuum or the sexual continuum would often be perceived as opinionated or snobbish; those who "overdo" domesticity would often be looked down on as dumb or "simple"; and the "oversexed" would be regarded as one or the other, either inferior or threatening in terms of intellect and etiquette and, in any case, destabilizing patriarchal hierarchies.

Arguably, women characters may change positionalities along the various continua, as can be seen in the study cases presented here, with antiheroines shifting from rejecting either domesticity or sexuality to pursuing them. Nevertheless, by fluctuating between the extremities of feminine performance and not adhering to one stable characterization as the exclusive fulfillment of femininity, the resisting antiheroine exposes the ideology that lies beneath the social construct that is femininity by pointing at its goldilocksian scrutiny.[14]

Chick TV Antiheroines

Despite the gender-exclusionary tones that governed discourses around antiheroism in the first decade of the twenty-first century, the late 2010s introduced scholarship that acknowledges the antiheroines of the 2000s American TV screen, recognizes their cultural significance, and explores their characterization (Tally 2016; Buonanno 2017; Haas, Pierce, and Busl 2020; Brost 2020; Pinedo 2021). Still, most of the analyses of antiheroic features in women characters on

---

14. For an elaborate positioning of the antiheroines analyzed in the book along the various continua, see the Appendix.

television have focused on the model that echoes that of men antiheroes by investigating antiheroines who stray morally, ethically, legally, or psychically, mostly in traditionally "masculine" genres.

This book is premised on the hypothesis that despite the characters seeming to be more easily "coronated" as antiheroic in acclaimed, perceivably masculine series (Warner in Mittell 2015b), complex antiheroinist figures are ubiquitous, even in undervalued pop, "chick" texts, challenging the social order no less (and perhaps even more so) than antiheroes in "masculine" texts. This notion is reflected in Nussbaum's (2013a) argument that the antiheroinism of *Sex and the City*'s (1998–2004) Carrie Bradshaw was not acknowledged as antiheroic due to the assumption that anything stylized (or formulaic, or pleasurable, or funny, or feminine, or explicit about sex rather than about violence, or made collaboratively) must be inferior." Antiheroism, Nussbaum suggests, is a label conventionally attached to characters in texts that are avant-garde, alienating, somber, masculine, explicit about violence rather than about sex, or auteurist, and is thereby more dependent on the tone of the text than on the de facto antiheroics expressed by its characters.

A feminist outlook on antiheroics may thus consider "feminine" or "stylized" texts in search of the social and cultural criticism that antiheroic characters invoke. This approach is also taken by Kristen Warner, who points at the disregard of soap operas as possible habitats for antiheroines, proclaiming that the genre has birthed many examples of antiheroines (or "proto" antiheroines) who are left out of the discourse regarding antiheroes, a discourse which continuously seeks to "legitimate" the legacy of antiheroes as rooted in texts that are "'masculine' and 'non-histrionically, soapy.'"[15] Significantly, War-

---

15. "We have tons of prime time and daytime soap characters who embody the essence (even at a 'proto' level) of women we love to hate who do what they do because they get off on causing havoc and yet also have feelings and want love and also to destroy everyone who has hurt them and maybe possesses mommy/daddy/social issues" (Warner, in Mittell 2015b).

ner draws attention to "the whiteness of anti-heroness," stressing that though women characters are not easily labeled antiheroines, women of color are even less likely to be given that status.

Nussbaum's and Warner's approaches spotlight antiheroism's gendered discursive constructedness, allowing for a new way of looking at the antiheroic in general and antiheroinism in particular—not only "misguided" (Martin 2013, 5) women in the background of "masculine" texts "toward masculine appeals" (Mittell 2015a, 150) but also resistant women in the front of "feminine" texts ("inferior," more "stylized," "soapy" chick TV).[16] Complex women characters can be traced back throughout the history of US women's television, but their complexities have grown gradually more sophisticated, apotheosized in the multilayered antiheroines of twenty-first-century television.

Initially, in the genesis of commercial television broadcasting in the United States, from the late 1940s throughout the 1950s, women were mostly "domesticated," even when leading television shows (mostly comedies at the medium's naissance, Edgerton 2007, 91–92). *I Love Lucy*'s (1951–57) Lucy, for example, "returns to her wifely and motherly duties at the end of every episode, keeping intact the myth of the nuclear family" (Edgerton 2007, 135). The 1950s narrative focused mainly on women adhering to social and gender decorum—such as June in *Leave It to Beaver* (1957–63) or Harriet in *The Adventures of Ozzie and Harriet*—or those who tried to challenge social and gender demands but were always eventually brought back into the binds of propriety, such as Lucy, or Gracie of *The George Burns and Gracie Allen Show* (1950–58). American 1950s televisual characterization of

---

16. Correspondingly, antiheroinist characters in genres traditionally identified with masculine sensibilities (such as crime, action, thriller, etc.) often bear a resemblance to men antiheroes (Buonanno 2017), mostly in terms of their crime-related moral ambiguity. In contrast, antiheroines in more "feminine" genres possess other, distinctively women-related antiheroinisms, as is elaborated in the following chapters.

women was arguably not oriented toward the antiheroic but, rather, maintained, at least declaratively, a conservative tone.[17]

The late 1960s and 1970s introduced a shift in American television by which television content providers tapped "into the social ferment of the times," as

> programs featuring working women, African American women, older women, divorced women, single mothers, and working-class women filled the 1970s home screen. *The Mary Tyler Moore Show*, *Rhoda*, *Good Times*, *The Jeffersons*, *Maude*, *One Day at a Time*, *Alice*, and *All in the Family* were prominent examples of the new fare. Controversial women's issues such as abortion, rape, equal employment opportunities, and racial and gender prejudice were featured subjects. At least in some prime-time programs, "woman," "women," and "femininity" were no longer conceived solely in terms of young, white, and middle-class characteristics. (D'Acci 1994, 14)

Inspired by the contemporaneous burst of what is known as the second wave of feminism, many of the depictions of women in the late 1960s and the 1970s presented characters who disputed hegemonic ideology, and scholarly analysis could certainly detect bouts of characterizational complexity in the period's representation of women. The era's development of the soap opera villainess could be seen as the "'proto' anti-heroine" (Warner, in Mittell 2015b), as these women try "to gain control over . . . feminine passivity" (Modleski 1979, 17) and express resistance to the demands of feminine performance, from Lisa in *As the World Turns* (1956–2010) to Katherine in *Dallas* (1978–91). Though representations in these decades were much more diverse, nonetheless "most of the social issues raised were domesticated—that is, they were represented as contained and resolvable at the level of the family" (D'Acci 1994, 14).

17. From the 1980s onward, researchers have reconsidered 1950s conservative television and have located subversive undertones. Patricia Mellencamp (1986), for example, has observed that Lucy's performative liberation negated her narrative subservience. Still, the predominant representational mode was conservative.

Conversely, the 1980s were marked as a decade of "backlash" (Faludi 1991) against the 1970s' feminist tendencies that accompanied the representation of women characters. According to Susan Faludi, the 1980s' political reactionary conservativism featured few women characters on television (155), "with sacrifice for one's husband and children once more a woman's highest calling" (1991, 179). Thus, if antiheroinism seemed to be imminent in the context of the diverse 1970s, an evaluation of the 1980s televisual landscape proves that said imminence was thwarted. In the 1980s, women characters were used as background or as means for the characterization of their male counterparts. The latter years of the decade, however, introduced another representational shift, "with women becoming more powerful in the 1980s and 1990s" (Spangler 2003, 9). Women-led shows in the late 1980s, such as *Roseanne* (1988–97), *Murphy Brown* (1988–98), and *Designing Women* (1986–93) shepherded a growing array of women characters who questioned ideology throughout the 1990s. What was more important, however, was that in the 1990s, complex, "flawed," or defiant women characters not only appeared in "the one television genre they had always called their own," namely, sitcoms (Faludi 1991, 155), but they also appeared in dramedies such as *Ally McBeal* (1997–2002) and *Sex and the City* (1998–2004); teen dramas and fantasy such as *Felicity* (1998–2002), *My So-Called Life* (1994–95), and *Buffy the Vampire Slayer* (1997–2003); and dramas such as *Sisters* (1991–96) and *Judging Amy* (1999–2005). By the end of the twentieth century, women characters were becoming more complex and resistant. Though they were still heroic in many ways—they usually strayed just a little along one of the antiheroinist continua—they began to push back against the qualities that women were expected to possess.

The 1990s also introduced the maturation of reality television into a full-fledged genre consisting of numerous subsets.[18] In keeping

---

18. US television has, of course, presented a lineup filled with unscripted programming since the early days of the medium, including news, sporting games, and various forms of television documentaries. Although several television texts were

with the turn of the twentieth century's representations of women in US television, the most prominent docusoap of the time, *The Real World* (1992–), featured women in myriad ways rather than as an essentialized mass, reflecting diverse systems of relationships between feminine performance and feminist resistance, with women intermittently displaying antiheroic characteristics. Turn of the millennium depictions of women in docusoaps aligned with those of women in scripted texts, such as *Ally McBeal*'s (1997–2002) Ally McBeal and *Sex and the City*'s (1998–2004) Carrie Bradshaw, with a characterization mode that aspired to the antiheroic (Nussbaum 2013a). Women characters at the turn of the century challenged hegemonic ideologies more explicitly than did their predecessors; though they were focalized protagonists, they would "push back against easy identification" (Nussbaum 2013b) as their comportment defied women's expected behavior. Thus, women characters of the late 1990s offered a reevaluation of the status quo, and each in her own way paved the way for the antiheroines of the 2000s.

In keeping with the growing complexity of television's women characters, twenty-first-century US television presents antiheroines who challenge social expectations (Marby 2006; Hohenstein and Thalmann 2019). Though scholarly work often distinguishes between the first decade of the twenty-first century and the second in terms of women's representation (Havas and Sulimma 2018; Hohenstein and Thalmann 2019), I see the second decade of the 2000s as continuing the development of antiheroinism that was planted in the early 2000s. This book thus looks at the critical point of the crystallization of antiheroinist characterization at the beginning of the twenty-first century—tied with the era's complex temporality—and traces its move toward the 2010s.

In outlining early twenty-first-century chick TV's convergence of antiher(oin)ism and complex temporality, I focus on shows that

---

retroactively labeled as reality shows, reality is commonly perceived to have emerged as a genre in the 1990s (Hill 2005).

debuted during the first decade and a half of the twenty-first century. The late 2010s have introduced chick TV texts that present the complex temporality-antiheroinist dyad, such as *Insecure* (2016–), *Better Things* (2016–), *Sorry for Your Loss* (2018–19), *Why Women Kill* (2019–), and others, but it is the early 2000s, in which the dynamic began to shape, that are the focus of this book. Of course, the periodization of the history of the representation of women on American television into phases is not clear cut, and exceptions obviously exist. Nevertheless, the dominant ways by which women have been represented in television history have been contingent on (whether in line with or against) the social zeitgeist of each era throughout the decades. Each decade therefore exhibits representational trends or dominances, and it is the early 2000s' tendencies I explore.

This book examines the antiheroinisms of Hannah Horvath, Bree Van de Kamp, Jackie Peyton, Mary Jane Paul, Meredith Grey, Cristina Yang, Brenda Chenowith, Claire Fisher, the Brown wives, and many of the stars of *The Real Housewives*, as these women are portrayed as self-absorbed, manipulative, bitchy, adulterous, unfriendly, unapologetic, and hysterical, to exhume chick TV antiheroines from the abyss of cultural dismissal.[19] The act of reclaiming their status as antiheroines reveals the radical and feminist potential of these complex and challenging "good-bad" women who struggle to negotiate the identity prescribed by social and gender demands of dominant ideology with their "experiences as subject" (Seel 2006).

---

19. Though this book reads many women's "bad" qualities as signs of resistance to order, it is important to note that other readings of such behaviors may see them as problematic from a humanistic point of view. For instance, Diane Negra (2009b) associates the negative characterizations that haunt many twenty-first-century women's cultural representations to be driven out of postfeminist, capitalistic conservativism; and Taylor Nygaard and Jorie Lagerwey (2020) correlate the performance of 2010s television's "horrible white people"—mostly women—to a zeitgeist of tone-deaf liberalism and white supremacy. However, as I do not aim to conduct a moral discussion of antiheroines' performance, I do not judge or condone their narcissistic, manipulative, deceitful, or otherwise depraved comportment. Rather, I observe it for its cultural and textual functions.

Time Unbound: Television Temporality and Feminist Thought

Temporal complexity has arguably become ubiquitous in twenty-first-century television (Ames 2012; Mittell 2006; Booth 2012; Kelly 2017; Shimpach 2010), manifesting itself in myriad ways. According to Ames,

> the most popular shows of the new millennium . . . play with time, slowing it down to unfold the narrative at rarely before seen rates (time retardation and compression) and disrupting the chronological flow itself (through the extensive use of flashbacks and the insistence that viewers be able to situate themselves in both the present and past narrative threads simultaneously). (2012, 8–9)

Drawing from Kelly (2012), Ames notes that US television texts in the 2000s lean toward "experimental temporality" and "temporal play" (Ames 2012, 13).

Though regarded as having reached a paramount level of sophistication in the twenty-first century, complex televisual temporality is often identified as having developed with the blurring of boundaries between episodicity and seriality, an amalgamation mostly considered to have started in the 1980s (Mittell 2006, though others, such as Levine and Newman 2012, find the process in earlier television texts). If, traditionally, most television was either episodic (sitcoms and most dramas, for example) or serial (soap operas), the 1980s saw a hybrid of seriality and episodicity, with series that presented episodic plots integrated with serial storytelling. This hybridity also introduced the first signs of breaking linearity insofar as shows such as *Dallas* (1978–91), *St. Elsewhere* (1982–88), or *Moonlighting* (1985–89) were both fragmentary and cumulative, both stalled and continuous. These and other shows also knowingly took up temporal play in contrast to the more temporally conservative, linear storylines of earlier decades and increasingly introduced dream sequences, fantasies, and reveries, which delayed the narrative flow, accelerated it, or slowed it down.

The following decades have seen more complex temporal structures, with flashbacks and flashforwards becoming staple forms (Ames 2012; Booth 2012) and various instances of delay and repetition punctuating television narrative (Creeber 2004).

The rising prevalence and intricacy of temporal play in twenty-first-century US television (Ames 2012) have been correlated with economic, industrial, and technological vicissitudes of the era (Ellis 2000; Johnson 2011; Mittell 2015a; Shimpach 2010; Booth 2011, 2012; Kelly 2017).[20] Such contexts notwithstanding, analyzing these complexities in line with their implications rather than their causes reveals the political power of television textuality.[21] Though the growing destabilization of narrative order—which has been traditionally based on linearity and causality—can be attributed to contextual shifts, television's complex temporality in the 2000s also coincides with a conceptual shift, a rhetoric "temporal turn," by which temporality is viewed as "a site of power and resistance . . . against the hegemony of universal time . . . with a particular focus on uncovering the relations between time, identity, futurity, and various forms of racialized, gendered, and sexual violence and agency" (Houdek and Phillips 2020).[22] Televisual resistance to narrative order can thus be read as resistance to social order—temporal complexity not only as a metaphoric or aesthetic structure affected by industry, economy, and

---

20. For contextual background regarding the rise of the 2000's US TV anti-heroines, see Tally (2016) and Pinedo (2021), who lay out backstage accounts and industrial factors regarding televisual flawed women characters and their creators.

21. The end of the 2010s saw dramatic transitions in economic, industrial, and technological contexts with the global 2020 pandemic and political and social upheavals in the United States and the world over. Though subsequent changes in the televisual landscape are expected—including to women's genres, women's characters, and textual temporality—as the writing of this book culminates in 2020, any attempts to delineate the nature of these changes would be speculative.

22. Surely, and as this book shows, temporality as a locus of power and potential resistance is not a twenty-first-century invention. Still, the perception of a "temporal turn" (Houdek and Phillips 2020) addresses a conceptual dominance.

technology but also as a political instrument. Within this framework, as this book demonstrates, when the feminist resistance of antiheroinism is joined with the narrative resistance of temporal complexity, the two constructs engender resistance not only to narrative order but also to social and patriarchal order.

The notion of resistance to conventional practices of time as related to resistance to the patriarchal order is reflected in the work of Judith Butler (1988), who stresses the correlation between repetition and gender performativity and points to the link between deviation from expected temporal practice and deviation from expected gender performance. Building on Butler's perception of gender as time-related performance (1990), Russell West-Pavlov notes that though perceived as natural, the concept of time is a human construct, ruled by interests and politics, serving ideologies, and "riddled with issues of power and hegemony" (2013, 3). The normative conception of time, namely, that it is a cultural construction, which Elizabeth Freeman refers to as "chrononormativity: causality, sequence, forward-moving agency, and so on" (2010, 64), "forms of temporal experience that seem natural to those whom they privilege" (3). Principally, if time is a hegemonic construct, then opposing its flow may signify opposition to hegemony itself.

The political significance of defamiliarizing and deconstructing temporal structures has been accordingly addressed by bearers of marginalized narratives, such as scholars of feminist studies (Kristeva 1981; Modleski 2002), critical race theory (Ganguly 2004; Streamas 2010), and queer politics (Halberstam 2005, Freeman 2010). Kristeva, for example, notes that "female subjectivity as it gives itself up to intuition becomes a problem with respect to a certain conception of time: time as project, teleology, linear and prospective unfolding; time as departure, progression, and arrival—in other words, the time of history" (1981, 17). Suggesting, then, that the linear time of history is in contention with "female subjectivity," Kristeva notes that nonlinear temporality has the power to reconsider women's marginalized narratives. Free from the sequentiality of historical time's "departure, progression, and arrival," temporal forms that eschew the teleological, the linear time of history, bear the potential to resist hegemony.

Similarly, the notion of alternative temporalities as spotlighting that which has been marginalized can be found in postcolonial criticism of hegemonic temporality as formulated by Keya Ganguly, who argues that "the postcolonial has been taken to represent an 'other' time whose logic and historical expression have been incommensurable with the normative temporalities of clock and calendar associated with western modernity" (2004, 162). Correspondingly, Halberstam suggests that "queerness" be perceived "as an outcome of strange temporalities, imaginative life schedules, and eccentric economic practices" (2005, 1).

Thus, "strange temporalities" (Halberstam 2005) that resist "chrononormativity" (Freeman 2010) and serve the marginalized voices of racial or sexual minorities can be found in cultural artifacts that foreground these voices (Houdek and Phillips 2020). In literature (Ricoeur 1990), film (Deleuze 1989; Turim 1989; Mroz 2012), and television (Fiske 1987; Mittell 2006), the resistance to time as linear, progressive, or coherent is manifested in the representation of events nonchronologically, in delays and accelerations, in reversals and repetitions, or in any textual form that challenges "chrononormativity." Depending on the ideological perspective of the text, the resistance of "temporal play" (Ames 2012) to narrative order and hegemonic temporality may also work to resist patriarchal order.[23] This book demon-

---

23. This book focuses on the feminist project that views temporal complexity as resistance to hegemonic order and "chrononormativity" as a construct, in contrast to the view of nonlinear temporality as connected to the rhythm and temporality of the female body interrelated with cyclicality and circularity (Mills, Pfeufer Kahn, Fox, in Johles Forman 1989; Ruddick 1990; Griffiths 1999). I thus concentrate on culture rather than on biology in a way that strives to circumvent classifications that perceive "'male time' and 'female time' as stable, dichotomous and biologically based categories" (Bryson 2007, 65), and which "can become essentialist, confirming dualistic, oppositional thinking" (122).

strates that when featured in chick TV, complex temporality promotes antiheroinist resistance to order.

Chick TV Temporality

This book hypothesizes that both complex antiheroinist figures and complex temporalities are ubiquitous in chick TV of the 2000s. Similarly to the way in which complex characters are more easily labeled antiheroes in stereotypically "masculine" texts, so is complex temporality more easily attributed to stereotypically "masculine" texts. It is telling that textual analyses of complex television temporality use many examples from many genres—from the comic *How I Met Your Mother* and *Arrested Development* (Mittell 2015a) and the dramatic *24* and *Lie to Me* (Shimpach 2010; Booth 2011), to science fiction shows such as *Supernatural* (Fuchs 2012), *Lost* (Johnson 2009; Mousoutzanis, in Laist 2011), and *Flashforward* (Kelly 2017). Seldom, however, do these analyses mention any women-led series, and even less so series that are considered as "women's genres."[24] I argue, in accordance with Nussbaum's (2013a) assertion, that the lack of academic writing on chick TV's temporal complexities is the result of "the assumption that anything stylized (or formulaic, or pleasurable, or funny, or feminine, or explicit about sex rather than about violence, or made collaboratively) must be inferior." The assumed inferiority of chick TV is tied with an assumed lack of complexity.

In writing about *Jane the Virgin* and its generic affiliation to telenovelas and "to other women's 'stories': the soap, the rom-com, the romance novel, and, more recently, reality television," Nussbaum states that "these are the genres that get dismissed as fluff." The dismissal of

---

24. Despite the dominant presence of women characters in a television series seeming to shape the way it is perceived (sometimes more than its genre does), women-led series that follow paradigms of men's genres seem to be more researched for their temporal complexities than are women-led chick TV. See, for example, Toni Pape (2012) on the suspense procedural *Damages*, or Kristi McDuffie (2012) on the supernatural police drama *Medium*.

these genres disregards any narrative complexity they might have, such as the multilayered narratives, reflexive metanarrativity, and generic hybridity found in *Jane the Virgin* (Nussbaum 2018). As in the case of other art forms in which women's texts were credited for their textual complexities—the woman's novel (Showalter 1977; Beer 1974), or the woman's film (Kaplan 1983; Modleski 2002), for example—the acknowledgment of women's television as narratively complex has been taken up by feminist scholars. Modleski (1979) has significantly asserted that the soap opera genre's stretched temporality is a political structure that offers resistance to narrative order, and Amanda Lotz has identified a lineage that runs from *The Days and Nights of Molly Dodd* (1987–88) to *Ally McBeal* and *Sex and the City*, pointing to a fundamental tie between "complex characterization, story, and style" (2006, 91). Mostly, however, soap operas and their "soapy" chick descendants have not been considered for their narrative complexities, stemming from the fact that "political unconsciousness has allowed the dominant, pro-masculinist discourse to devalue the soap opera as a nonaesthetic" (Blumenthal 1997, 91).

This notion is not new, of course, and could be traced back to Virginia Woolf in 1929, who noted in *A Room of One's Own* that

> Speaking crudely, football and sport are "important"; the worship of fashion, the buying of clothes "trivial". And these values are inevitably transferred from life to fiction. This is an important book, the critic assumes, because it deals with war. This is an insignificant book because it deals with the feelings of women in a drawing-room. A scene in a battle-field is more important than a scene in a shop—everywhere and much more subtly the difference of value persists. (2000, 74)

Historically, and in a sense also contemporarily, "chick" issues and texts have been considered trivial and superficial, that is, the opposite of complex.

Of course, many chick texts have been subjects of academic studies, and most of the series analyzed in this book have been researched.

Books dedicated to *Girls*, *Six Feet Under*, *The Real Housewives*, *Desperate Housewives*, and *Grey's Anatomy* as well as numerous academic papers on each of the case studies in this book address themes, representation, and genre. Still, chick TV series are usually absent in researches on narrative, textual, or temporal complexities. This book sets out to examine the narrative and textual temporalities of *Girls, Being Mary Jane, Nurse Jackie, Grey's Anatomy, Six Feet Under, Desperate Housewives, The Real Housewives, and Sister Wives*—as they delay the narrative, rewind or fast-forward it, stretch and expand it, break or repeat it—to redeem chick TV temporality from its supposed artlessness. The act of reclaiming chick TV's temporal complexities reveals their radical and feminist potential to challenge order.

Not only do I maintain that chick TV's temporality and women characters are more complex than often acknowledged, I also posit that twenty-first-century chick TV features complex temporality that is linked to complex antiheroines. This tie between temporal and antiheroinist complexities constructs twenty-first-century chick TV's challenge to order. The following chapters are divided according to the layers of temporal-antiheroinist challenges to hegemonic order: *resistance*, focusing on antiheroinist resistance that is correlated with intradiegetic devices' temporal delay of the narrative; *deviation*, focusing on antiheroinism that is correlated with the flashback, flashforward, and flash-sideways' deviation from the narrative; *serialization*, focusing on antiheroinism that is correlated with the serialization of resistances to narrative order; and *rewriting*, focusing on antiheroinism that is correlated with intertextual repetition that rewrites the narrative order.

Chapter 1, "Resistance," addresses the basic resistance that the tie between temporality and antiheroines may offer. It explores literary devices that imply a play with time—such as story-within-story, reverie and fantasy, and docusoap confessionals—correlated with the character of the antiheroine and her feminist resistance. Using *Girls* as a primary case study, with comparative analyses of *Nurse Jackie*, *Six Feet Under*, and *Being Mary Jane*, the chapter examines the series' use of intradiegetic devices that implicitly work to delay narrative chrononormativity and antiheroinize their women protagonists, thereby resisting order.

Chapter 2, "Deviation," analyzes temporal constructions in the architecture of television episodes, focusing on flashbacks, flashforwards, and flash-sideways. I argue that these temporal forms not only resist order but also work to deviate from and disrupt the hegemonic flow, as well as create potential for alternative temporal spaces. These constructs are examined vis-à-vis the antiheroines' notions of their futures and pasts, imagined and real worlds. The chapter centers on *Grey's Anatomy*, with comparative analyses of *Desperate Housewives* and *Six Feet Under*, and strives to ascertain the link between textual temporal complexity and antiheroinism that not only implicitly promotes resistance to hegemonic time and culture but also explicitly deviates from it.

Chapter 3, "Serialization," looks at the televisual serial form from the perspective of its work with and contribution to antiheroinism. Tracing the form's feminist tradition, from soap operas' stretching seriality to contemporary serialized chick TV narratives, the chapter focuses on the ties between the temporalities of the serial form, women's texts, and feminist resistance. The chapter's central case study is the docusoap franchise *The Real Housewives*, examined for the antiheroinism of its cast members as correlated with the series' form of seriality. The reading of *The Real Housewives* through its seriality demonstrates the power of feminist textual analysis to challenge viewpoints communicated through plot.

Chapter 4, the final chapter, "Rewriting," demonstrates the manner in which narrative resistance, episodic deviation, and complex serialization work to rewrite an alternative temporality—alternative to the hegemonic time flow and to the hegemonic social order. The section focuses on the links between antiheroines in television serials through reflexive intertextual repetitions across various televisual texts. The main study case is *Desperate Housewives*, with comparative analyses of *Nurse Jackie, Being Mary Jane, Grey's Anatomy, Six Feet Under, Girls, Sister Wives*, and references to past and contemporaneous chick TV. These analyses support the hypothesis that intertextual repetitions across antiheroine narratives in chick TV bolster antiheroinist resistance and thus rewrite the dominant order.

The "Conclusion" charts the models of complex temporality and antiheroinism derived from the analyses in the chapters. In reviewing chick TV's temporal layers and forms of antiheroinism, the conclusion spotlights the ways in which early twenty-first-century chick TV in the United States proposes a different interrelation with historical linear time and patriarchal heroics and focuses on the radical potential of the antiheroinism-temporality dyad—feminist resistance to narrative and patriarchal order. *Chick TV: Antiheroines and Time Unbound* proposes a reading of antiheroines as defined by their correlation with the textual complexities in which their stories are told. By looking to "see, rather than just see through . . . form" (Joyrich 2004, 190)—in this case the form of chick TV—this book correlates chick TV's textual feminist resistance of complex temporality with the characterizational feminist resistance of antiheroinism.

1
Resistance

In investigating antiheroinism and textual temporality and their potential to disrupt patriarchal order, I focus on the notion that resistance to temporal progression is a resistance to strive toward a future—at least in the hegemonic materialization of a future—age-appropriate life decisions and adherence to expected familial and social experiences. This notion is articulated by J. Halberstam as an aspiration toward "strange temporalities, imaginative life schedules, and eccentric economic practices" (2005, 1), all challenging chrononormativity.

The Feminist Resistance of Temporal Delay

This challenge to chrononormativity is closely related to the effect of televisual complex temporality on characterization, as indicated by Gillian Silverman and Sarah Hagelin, who argue that the 2010s antiheroine "sidesteps the mandate of futurity (the female subject oriented toward progress and development) in favor of presentism and in-the-moment sensation" (2018, 881). The insistence on holding on to a present rather than aspiring toward a future is exposed in both antiheroines' conduct and in the texts' unfolding.

Temporal play that works to challenge identity and characterization is present in non-chick TV series, from the supernatural *Supernatural* to the sitcom *How I Met Your Mother* or the animation satire *South Park*.[1] Paul Booth notes that

---

1. The temporality of all these texts is addressed by Melissa Ames (2012).

> Jumps in temporality based on a metaphoric character's motivations function to offer the character a chance to facilitate a greater understanding of his/her own life through reflection, self-awareness, or comparison with others. . . . Ultimately, temporal displacement becomes one more way that contemporary complex television narratives function as both a means for and representation of a fracturing of personal identity. (2012, 101)

However, as I intend to demonstrate, when coupled with chick TV, "temporal displacement" promotes a character's understanding of the self and also drives (women) characters to resist order.

Reclaiming Antiheroinism through Intradiegetic Resistance

The first layer of temporality I examine is the intradiegetic level with narrative devices that delay the progress of the narrative temporal flow toward the future and thus insist on "presentism and in-the-moment sensation" (Silverman and Hagelin 2018, 881).[2] Such intradiegetic devices, such as story-within-story, dream, or reverie, pause the narrative as they shift to a different, inner, ontological level of narration (Chen 2008, 399). Though the plotline picks up where it was paused before the intradiegesic fissure, as Fanfan Chen notes, the intradiegesis generates transformation in the diegesis. In chick TV, the intradiegesis inscribes its resistance to temporal progression on the narrative, manifested in antiheroinist resistance, as can be seen in the following analyses of *Girls*, *Nurse Jackie*, and *Being Mary Jane*.

Girls: *Resisting via Story-within-Story*

The following discussion of the intradiegetic devices in *Girls* focuses on the way that the temporal delay offered by the show's story-within-story works to characterize the protagonist's antiheroinism and injects

---

2. I use the term "flow" to denote movement or progression of a particular television text and not to refer to the flow between television texts in the context of production and viewership analysis as offered by Raymond Williams (1974).

a form of feminist resistance into the diegetic text. *Girls* is very much about girls, rather young women, and though it was produced by the acclaimed HBO with an up-and-coming creator (Lena Dunham, the star of the show, is also the creator), its focus on the romantic, sexual, social, and to some extent professional lives of young women renders its chick TV affiliation. The series' protagonist Hannah is an aspiring writer, and her knack for storytelling is dominant in the plot, as she writes and tells stories and sometimes fabricates lies. The show thus occasionally dives into intradiegetic story-within-story techniques, thereby delaying narrative progression. One such instance occurs in the first season's ninth episode, "Leave Me Alone," in which Hanna is invited to present her writing in a public reading. She decides to read an essay about a guy she liked in college who turned out to be a hoarder. "I slept in his dorm room on top of a pile of collapsed Chinese food boxes like a semester's worth," she tells Ray, a friend and the manager of a café where she works. "I don't know if that sounds really trivial to you," she utters, adding, "it's definitely supposed to be funny; it's not supposed to be super serious, but it's also supposed to take on bigger issues, like fear of intimacy—" at which point Ray interrupts, insisting: "What in the world could be more trivial than intimacy?" (*Girls*, "Leave Me Alone").

Ray stresses that it is exactly the theme with which Hannah attempts to defend her storyline that is triviality apotheosized, as he distinguishes it from "real" issues, such as

> cultural criticism. How about years of neglect and abuse? How about acid rain? How about the plight of the giant panda bear? How about racial profiling? How about urban sprawl? How about divorce? How about death? How about death? Death is the most fucking real. You should write about death. That's what you should write about. Explore that. Death. (*Girls*, "Leave Me Alone")

Even more so than "cultural criticism" and various environmental concerns, that is, what Ray perceives to be the ultimate "real" subject matter is death. That juxtaposition, between intimacy—here trivialized—and death—here elevated—draws a clear line between themes that are worthy of exploration and those that are not. For Hannah, however, intimacy is a major issue, as she points out, implicitly endorsing the notion that relationships and friendships encompass profundities interesting enough to explore. Ray's criticism is nevertheless disorienting for her and, coupled with others' criticism, eventually leads her to present a different piece at the reading—an essay that fittingly focuses on death.

The division between "worthy" and "unworthy" themes thus overcomes Hannah's initial creative drive, and she ostensibly abandons the "trivial" subject matter of intimacy in favor of the "real" subject matter of death. Still, Hannah's death-related story within the story of "Leave Me Alone" does not delineate an existential study of the human condition vis-à-vis mortality. Rather, it unfolds the specificities of the protagonist's experience when a boy she had met in a chat room died, and the brief reading that is presented in the episode (only the first few sentences of the essay are represented on screen) is not at all devoid of "trivial" details:

> I met Igor online in a chat room for fans of an obscure punk band my vegan friend Marina liked. Igor's screen name was "pyro000," which belied a level of articulation unusual for an internet boyfriend. So he became my internet boyfriend for six blissful months, until his friend IM'd me to say that he had died. Died. (*Girls*, "Leave Me Alone")

Though Hannah reiterates, perhaps for dramatic effect, the fact that her boyfriend has died, the majority of the exposition features seemingly mundane details far removed from the "real" seriousness that a theme such as death seems to require. Most of the excerpt consists of mapping the strain of emotional attachments that led the narrator to Igor, focusing on her friend Marina—including Marina's diet and her musical preferences—in much greater detail than on the circumstances of Igor's death.[3]

---

3. Interestingly, in the memoir of Lena Dunham, the creator of *Girls*, a chapter titled "Igor: Or, My Internet Boyfriend Died and So Can Yours" tells a similar story,

Even when addressing the serious issue of death, that is, Hannah does so as a supplement to that which is considered trivial rather than as the nucleus of the text, thereby calling attention back to the so-called trivial, in this case popular culture and intricacies of friendships and relationships. By repeating the story-within-story as a device that insists on placing the "trivial" in the foreground of narrative, the episode subtextually refuses to perpetuate textual conventions that vilipend women's stories. More so than that, the way in which *Girls* represents the "trivial" becomes a mechanism of feminist politics in and of itself as the episode depicts traditionally "important" or "real" themes. Thus, the episode ostensibly reinforces the distinction between "the male and the female, the serious and the frivolous" (Bourdieu 1984, 93–94). However, it does so in a way that uses said "important" and "real" themes as vehicles to explore issues considered feminine and trivial, such as intimacy, emotionality, and friendship, rather than as subject matters that are explored on their own merits. The "real," that is, is used as a means to the "trivial" and not for its own sake.[4] The work of the intradiegetic device of story-within-story, which delays temporal progression to invert the hierarchy presented in the diegesis between "real" (that is men's) issues and "trivial" (that is women's) issues in "Leave me Alone" is relevant to *Girls*' position as chick TV, a subgenre for which marginalization and devaluation is part of its political power. Chick TV's insistence

---

one of meeting Igor in a chat room and later hearing he had passed away. Though the book's version of the narrative is much more extended compared to the excerpt presented in the fictionalized televisual reading, Igor similarly appears at a later stage in the story rather than in its beginning (despite him being the subject of the chapter), and his character is introduced only after a detailed account of how Dunham's school—and later her parents—purchased computers and a description of women friends sharing chat room experiences (Dunham 2014, 24–32).

4. The textual inversion utilized by *Girls* in its harnessing of "major" issues (and thus major language) in order to focus on women's trivialized issues echoes Deleuze's and Guattari's concept of "minor literature" in its "setting up a minor practice of major language from within" (1986, 18).

on women's concerns is a form of feminist resistance to the cultural regulation of that which is considered important. The temporal delay promoted by the story-within-story offers a "feminist-inspired reworking of what counts as legitimate public discussion" (Gamson 1998, 6) in its resistance to allow the diegesis to progress toward a future that continuously perpetuates the existing social order. Hannah's insistence on women's culture in the story-within-story features an implied antiheroinism as her feminist resistance is not evident in the text as much as it is revealed in the intradiegetic temporal/ontological level.

Girls' intradiegetic devices that work to delay the narrative flow and inject feminist resistance into the diegesis are scattered throughout as the series is rife with "metatextual commentary" (Grdešić 2013). In the episode "Dead Inside" (season 3, episode 4), Hannah spends an afternoon with her neighbor and her boyfriend's sister Caroline. Caroline tells a story about her and Adam's cousin, who died of muscular dystrophy when she was twelve years old—a story she then confesses to have made up. The made-up, albeit highly intricate, intradiegetic story about the fake cousin Margaret is again not staged for the sake of debating decay of the body or fear of mortality. Caroline's story not only serves to test Hannah's response but is also later retold by Hannah as she recounts it to Adam, this time she as the bearer of the lie. Thus, the story is introduced in the episode for the sake of studying the value of honesty in relationships and the signification of sensitivity. Here, again, the story-within-story inserts a feminist resistance to the marginalization of women's issues into the diegesis.

That resistance works to reveal that the category of triviality is a gendered construct and exposes its formulation as such. By using traditionally "important" themes as instruments for destabilizing a "symbolic order that polices and reinforces gender hierarchy and identity" (Drucilla Cornell, in Pheng Cheah et al. 1998, 24), *Girls* calls into question normalized social constructs, their gender-based classification, and "the criteria that . . . determine the artistic and social merit of creative expressions" (Rakow 1986, 32). I thus argue that *Girls*' cultural and feminist significance stems from, among other things, its resistance to the dismissal of that which is considered feminine and its foregrounding of marginalized and trivialized issues in women's lives, thus insisting that the "feelings of women" matter as Virginia Woolf asserted in 1929 in *A Room of One's Own*. Hannah's antiheroinist narcissism, which Ray classifies as an act of antisocial disorder, is actually a social disorder as Hannah's hated personality trait in the diegesis becomes a symbol of feminist resistance to the social order in the intradiegetic story-within-story. The story-within-story thus reinterprets her culturally castigated narcissism into antiheroinism in a resistance to adhere to the cultural prioritization of "major," that is, men's, issues.

Nurse Jackie: *Resisting via Voice-Over and Reverie*

The analysis of *Girls* demonstrates the power of intradiegetic temporality to offer feminist resistance when inhabited by an antiheroine. The intradiegetic delay of narrative temporality implies a resistance to hegemonic time and order that insists on "feminine" culture, effecting a culturally resisting antiheroine, one who defies patriarchal culture by favoring women's culture and whose antiheroinism is revealed through textual reading. This antiheroinist resistance is thus not necessarily overt in the text itself but, rather, covertly hidden in the creases of the text, exhumed by a close feminist reading, as the one analyzing the story-within-story in *Girls*. Next, I read other textual devices that covertly work to delay the temporal flow, such as voice-over, reverie, or dream in *Nurse Jackie* (2009–15), illustrating that when these devices are introduced in an antiheroinist chick TV text, they work to offer feminist resistance.

Nurse Jackie, also a twenty-first-century chick TV dramedy, often features reveries by its titular character. The series follows Jackie, a nurse who is a married mother of two but keeps her family life a secret at work by posing as a single childless woman (and having an affair with the hospital pharmacist). Led by a woman protagonist and focusing on the dramas of her domestic, professional, sexual, and social life, *Nurse Jackie* corresponds with the generic affiliation of chick TV.

More explicitly antiheroinist, Jackie plays two roles: at home she is the forty-something woman who fulfills patriarchal expectations to have a family and, at work, she pretends to be single and childless, has an affair, and abuses prescription drugs. By playing this double role, Jackie brings her adherence to and rejection of chrononormative "life schedules" (Halberstam 2005, 1) to the foreground, correlating temporally governed signs (age, fertility, body) with social compliance and resistance (Negra 2009a), that is, antiheroinism.

Both *Nurse Jackie* the text and nurse Jackie the character seem to delay temporal progression and remain in the present. At the end of the pilot episode, Jackie is seen entering her home as her voice-over is heard saying, "if I were a saint, which maybe I want to be, which maybe I don't, I would be like Augustine. He knew there was good in him and he knew there was some not so good. And he wasn't going to give up his earthly pleasures before he was good and ready. 'Make me good, God, but not yet'" (pilot).[5] Jackie portrays an expected aspiration toward a future of mending her improper ways but opts for stalling said future. She desires to remain in the "not yet," that is, to avoid the forward thrust of the patriarchal "time of history" (Kristeva 1981, 17) and antiheroinistically linger in the temporal dimension that enables her impropriety.

The voice-over serves protagonist Jackie's inner voice as "a prime means of making viewers aware of the subjectivity of perception (focalization) and storytelling (narration)" (Kozloff 1988, 62). Thus, though Jackie serves as a homodiegetic narrator ("the narrator present as a character in the story he tells" [Genette 1980, 245]), the voice-over is positioned in a separate ontological dimension from that of the unfolding events as it is delivered directly to the viewers without

---

5. This voice-over is delivered during the final scene of the pilot, in which Jackie's home life is revealed. After having been characterized as a single workaholic throughout the episode, Jackie's entrance into her home in this final scene shows her greeting a husband and two children. The true nature of her workplace persona is kept secret, reflected by her stepping into a corridor shadow at the end of the aforementioned monologue.

the knowledge of characters other than Jackie. The voice-over in the scene hence serves as a dual temporal state—a longing to halt progression in its content and an omnitemporal or sur-temporal commentarial dimension in its diegetic positioning. The voice-over device thus expands the story time into a temporal dimension that includes both no-time and all-time, thereby not only delaying but also challenging the diegesis's ostensibly progressive movement. Here the voice-over works similarly to the story-within-story in *Girls*—a separate, though part of the story world, ontological realm that works to challenge hegemonic social values. Such intradiegetic devices—story-within-story for Hannah and the voice-over for Jackie—serve as reflections of both characters' inner worlds, their antiheroinist aspirations to bring forth their own moral, social, and temporal perceptions, celebrated through the text itself even if not fully expressed in the diegesis.

The delay of the diegetic temporal flow for intradiegetic textual resistance is manifested through several other devices in *Nurse Jackie* that are used to express Jackie's inner self. Those instances are not entirely disconnected from the narrative flow, as Jackie is addicted to prescription drugs and therefore slips into drug-induced hallucinations, reveries, and dreams. This "drug time," so to speak, stalls the movement of time and carries her into dream-like scenarios, thereby keeping Jackie, as she willed it, in the "not yet," in the present. In one such scene in the first season finale (season 1, episode 12, "Health Care & Cinema"), Jackie imagines the stereotypical American home in an animated image of a suburban cottage with her husband and two daughters in front of it as she, lying on the floor due to a stress-related, drug-catalyzed breakdown she had undergone before the reverie struck upon her, is wearing a mid-twentieth-century nurse's outfit. This blissful scene demonstrates the social image of home and family to which Jackie is expected to aspire. However, seeing as the scene is depicted as a hallucination and is in fact the opposite of Jackie's life (in which her addiction alienates her family members and she is far from the image of perfect mother), it stresses her failure to fulfill that image and her clinging to the present time and to antiheroinism on the domestic continuum.

This scene exemplifies the stepping-out-of-time so badly needed for Jackie, both in terms of stepping out of the expected adherence to life schedules (Halberstam 2005) and in terms of stepping out of the linear temporal progression of her reality. By pausing the diegesis in favor of a surreal image of the perfect heteronormative, chrononormative patriarchal order, the narrative positions Jackie as resisting order when the diegesis is resumed.

Six Feet Under: *Resisting via Fantasy Sequences*

Intradiegetic devices that covertly antiheroinize its women characters can be found in various chick TV scenes of reverie and dream. Of course, fantasy sequences in otherwise realistically inclined television texts are neither unique to chick TV nor to twenty-first-century television. Glen Creeber addresses "social surrealism" as a television mode of address that "appears to more accurately reflect the social inconsistencies and moral uncertainties of a 'postmodern' world" (2004, 15). More specifically, fantasy sequences in otherwise realistic stories are usually associated with quality television (McCabe and Akass 2007). Nevertheless, such sequences can be found in chick TV, as in *The Days and Nights of Molly Dodd* (1987–88) and *My So-Called Life* (1994–95), and, following the popularization of the trope by the turn-of-the-millennium *Ally McBeal* (Nochimson 2000; Smith 2007), they have become more prevalent in twenty-first-century chick TV. Additionally, and more so than in other genres, the incorporation of fantasy sequences in chick TV offers a politicized aspect to a perceivably apolitical text. By creating holes in the progression of the narrative flow, instances of "social surrealism" not only reflect a destabilized order, as observed by Creeber, but also further destabilize it, that is, antiheroinistically resisting it.

The hybrid quality-chick *Six Feet Under* exemplifies the difference between men's fantasies, which lean toward more "serious" issues, such as faith and death, and correlate with "men's genres," and women's fantasies, which are more associated with chick-related issues, such as relationships, family, domesticity, and sex.[6] *Six Feet Under* follows the Fisher family, who own a funeral home and also live in one, as the funeral services are run from the family home basement. The series is both explicitly complex (Mittell 2015a; McCabe and Akass 2007) and chick TV (which is usually more implicitly complex) as it presents a dominant presence of women characters and draws much of its generic orientation from soap operas in its focus on dialogue, family, relationships, and articulates women's subjectivity.[7] Reverie and fantasy are ubiquitous in the series. A significant example of intradiegetic pauses for reverie or fantasy is manifested in social conflicts and self-conflicts presented through imagined encounters with images of the dead conversing and interacting with the living. Like the intradiegetic reverie, the fantastical appearance of the dead is not a science-fiction-like characteristic but, rather, an aesthetic technique of materializing inner dialogues as a way to personify and express the conflicts of a living character. However, though all the lead ensemble characters in the series experience such fantasies, the fantasies of the women characters work to antiheroinize the women and destabilize and renegotiate their identities. Whereas the men's fantasies work to help them come to terms with some inner truth that is to be revealed—David's fantasies help him come to terms with the contradiction between his religious faith and his homosexuality, and Nate's fantasies help him come to terms with the conflict between his romanticism and his need for solipsism—the women's fantasies effect change.

Six Feet Under's three main women characters are Ruth, the family matriarch; Brenda, the on-and-off girlfriend and later wife of Nate, Ruth's eldest son; and Claire, Ruth's daughter and Brenda's sister-in-law.

---

6. Both quality and chick are, of course, discursive definitions and are not necessarily contradictory. *Six Feet Under*'s genre hybridity is highly tangled, and the men are very preoccupied with relationships, family, and sex. Nevertheless, I find a distinction between their characterization and the women's characterization through intradiegetic devices.

7. See also Glen Creeber's writing on the hybridity of "soap drama" (2004, 116).

These women's fantastical encounters with images of the dead drive them to renegotiate their performance of femininity, specifically along the sexual and domestic antiheroinist continua. Ruth's encounters with the spirit of her dead husband propel her into a "journey towards a new symbolic role" (Akass 2005, 120) that resists the immersion in motherhood and domesticity to which she has become accustomed during her married life. Instead, she discovers her sexuality, new friendships, and positions in the world and is essentially antiheroinized.

Similarly, Claire's imagined conversation with her deceased father engenders identity renegotiation, and Brenda's vision of a conversation with her soon-to-be-husband's dead wife leads her to reconstruct her identity. In the conversation, elaborated in this book's final chapter "Rewriting," Brenda processes a miscarriage she has undergone, realizing that she is able to antiheroinistically contain multiplicities: being a sexual subject who also possesses maternal inclinations and resists the traditional Madonna/whore dichotomy by actively blurring the lines. The fantastical intradiegetic pause effects a renegotiation of her feminine performance, resisting the cultural dichotomy of patriarchal order by constructing a subjectivity that is open to "accommodate ambiguity and . . . multiple positionalities: . . . exploring more than defining, searching more than arriving" (Walker 1995).[8] The women of *Six Feet Under* are thus antiheroinized via "representational forms that understand subjectivity as about process rather than identity" (Akass 2005, 132–33). Among these representational forms are intradiegetic devices that pause the narrative to reconsider order and textually resist it.

Being Mary Jane: *Resisting via "Live" Segments*

An even more covert representational form that destabilizes temporal and patriarchal order can be found in shifts in stylistic language "hiding" in the design of the mise-en-scène. A significant example of the

---

8. This quote is taken from Rebecca Walker's writing on Third Wave feminism and "third wave subjectivity" (1995).

use of visual codes to destabilize narrative order is *Being Mary Jane*'s use of "live television" aesthetics to distinguish a distinct "now" from its surrounding time flow. *Being Mary Jane* (2013–19) follows Mary Jane Paul, an acclaimed TV news anchor struggling with love and family. The series amalgamates single-city-girl shows from *Mary Tyler Moore* to *Sex and the City* in characterizing Mary Jane as career driven and looking for love with the tradition of Black women's shows by centering the subjectivity of Black lead Mary Jane.[9] The soap-operatic narrative—in focusing on dialogue, family, and relationships—positions *Being Mary Jane* as a protagonist-led chick TV text. Given that Mary Jane is a news anchor, parts of the depictions of her news show are marked as "live." The series thus distinguishes between two levels of television fiction: the temporal flow of the plot with the "live" segments that bear "live" stylistics and a fictionalized, scripted version of a live news show.

The "live" segments are stylized differently from the main narrative, thus bisecting the narrative: the news representation of Mary Jane as anchor and the exposure of the backstage of the news production. The same scene can be captured from the point of view of the viewers who watch Mary Jane deliver the news and from a point of view inside the studio, the former accompanied by network captions and the latter exposing the studio equipment. The "liveness" works in a similar manner to the story-within-story as a delay to the text's temporal progression. In a sense, it is a story-within-story, as the segments are not directly related to the narrative, though they are often thematized to resonate with issues with which Mary Jane is struggling. The frame stylization departs from the series' predominant mode of address, drawing attention to splitting and delaying of the narrative flow. In *Being Mary Jane*, the "live" stories often revolve around women's issues, particularly women of color, and the delay of story in favor of a lingering on issues regarding Black women's beauty, procreation,

---

9. *Being Mary Jane*'s creator, Mara Brock Akil, has consistently articulated Black women's subjectivity in her work, including *Girlfriends* (2000–2008) and *The Game* (2006–15).

and other performative forms of femininity, works to resist chrononormativity both by insisting on a perpetual present and by introducing women's resistances.

In the fifth episode of the second season of *Being Mary Jane* ("No Eggspectations"), Mary Jane hosts a current affairs segment titled "Modern Day Motherhood" in which she performs as both reporter and the subject of her own reportage work as she is undergoing an egg-freezing process. Her visit to the fertility doctor is stylized as live shooting with a hand-held camera framing the scene, the diegetic news show caption at the bottom of the screen, and Mary Jane directly facing the camera to address her audience. During the live segment, Mary Jane receives bad news as the doctor informs her that her follicles are in worse shape than expected. As soon as she breaks for commercials, Mary Jane—now stylized differently, with the frame tighter and more stable and the caption gone—loses her professional poise and distressingly questions the doctor about what might have gone wrong. While the character of Mary Jane is often conflicted about social certainties and antiheroinistically challenges gender expectations (she is not certain she is interested in having children, for example, but nonetheless undertakes fertility consults), the "live" segment features her as conforming to what is expected of her as a woman—seeking to fulfill motherhood and conducting herself with poise and calm.

The ontological splitting features Mary Jane both performing proper femininity and resisting it. The splitting hence positions Mary Jane vis-à-vis gender performative demands, demonstrating that adherence to these demands varies according to circumstances, thereby rendering social demands arbitrary and constructed. Following this stylistic ontological split, Mary Jane will antiheroinistically reexamine "handed down assumptions" (Brombert 1999) regarding feminine performance, specifically along the domestic, sexual, and class antiheroinist continua, thereby negotiating her subjectivity (Seel 2006).[10]

---

10. Class is problematized in the representation of Black women, who are faced with intersectional policing vis-à-vis "politics of respectability" (Brooks Higginbotham 1993).

Another stylistic shift occurs in *Being Mary Jane*'s season 2, episode 9 ("Line in the Sand"), which similarly complicates the present tense by oscillating between "live" stylistics and diegetic stylistics. This time, the "live" segment follows a panel Mary Jane hosts about Black women's beauty, again highlighting issues of gender performance, including issues of race. The segment references an extradiegetic controversy spurred by evolutionary psychologist Satoshi Kanazawa's attempt to harness biological parameters to claim that Black women are less physically attractive than women of other ethnicities (2011). The *Being Mary Jane* segment features extradiegetic experts, rather than actors playing experts, who deliberate about the racist atmosphere against Black women's bodies as apotheosized by Kanazawa's inflammatory claims. Here, again, as in "No Eggspectations," the stylization of the sequence shifts between live framing, marked with the news show captions and panel participants looking straight at the camera, and diegetic framing, capturing the studio cameras and thus exposing the mechanism of the studio on the one hand but invisible to the panel participants on the other.

The "live" segment, both extradiegetic in the presence of social commentators speaking as themselves rather than acting and intradiegetic in the delay of the "live" story-within-story pause of narrative progression, presents a split ontological layer in the text. The extradiegetic incendiary text regarding Black women's beauty serves as an intradiegetic vantage point for exposing the constructedness of femininity, Blackness, and beauty. By addressing the social marginalization of Black women and the devaluation of their bodies, the panel injects defamiliarization of racial and gendered hierarchies into the text. Although the *Being Mary Jane* finale concludes in a traditional return to order with Mary Jane marrying the man she loves, the series introduces several instances of resistance and antiheroinism as Mary Jane refuses to take social constructs for granted. "I don't think I want to get married," Mary Jane tells a friend in the first season's second episode ("Girls Night In"). "It may not be for me. Maybe marriage is just something I say I want because I'm supposed to say it. You know? Like I'm a damn trained seal." While Mary Jane pursues romantic union and family, she also doubts them. The use of intradiegetic shifts in style and encoding toward "live" aesthetics pauses the narrative movement toward final resolution and return to order by questioning the naturalization of order. Thus, through fissures and creases in the diegesis, the text of *Being Mary Jane* antiheroinizes the titular protagonist.

The intradiegetic device that splits the narrative ontology through the verisimilitude of liveness has been featured in television from *Goodnight, Beantown* (1983–84) to *Studio 60 on the Sunset Strip* (2006–7), *The Newsroom* (2012–14), and *The Morning Show* (2019–) and in women-led shows, mostly sitcoms, from *The Mary Tyler Moore Show* (1970–77) to *Murphy Brown* (1988–2018) and *30 Rock* (2006–13). As many scholars have noted, liveness is a distinguishing element of television, reflecting its immediacy and timeliness (Feuer 1983; Spigel 1992; Levine 2008). However, by representing liveness rather than representing through liveness, reflexive television about television liveness depicts ontological divergences that defamiliarize television's representational encoding strategies (Barker 1988, drawing from Hall 1980) and destabilize narrative order. It is the way in which Mary Jane's subjectivity and resistance are not only incorporated in the representation of liveness (as is also the case in *Murphy Brown*, for example) but are also reconstructed by it, fueling both feminist and racial resistance, that makes *Being Mary Jane* a compelling case study for antiheroinization through the intradiegetic pause of "liveness."

The Docusoap: Resisting via the Confessional

Intradiegetic devices that work to pause the narrative and open potential for resisting order also appear in the storytelling mechanism of docusoaps. This is most evident in reality television's staple confessional/testimonial convention—the retrospective comments of cast members on an event unfolding in the diegetic "present" are interwoven into the narrative. A scene following one's experience would be injected with one's later (sometimes months later) comments on the experience, as one speaks directly to the camera, now with the wisdom of hindsight, on a past event represented to viewers as the narrative "now." The confessional is effectively an intradiegetic device that disrupts narrative temporality, thereby delaying the narrative flow for a separate diegetic layer that is a future in relation to the diegetic present but is incorporated into the story.

Consequently, the confessional signifies a split in the diegetic flow, unfolding both a limited subjective level of narration and an informed, albeit still subjective and potentially unreliable, level of narration. Emma Lieber notes that the reality confessional captures participants as both objects (their stories are featured) and subjects (they are given voice to narrate these stories as they are told) and as both "inhabiting time" (as characters in the stories) and "outside of it" (as narrators in the confessionals) (2013, 124). Thus, the confessional signifies a split that is both ontological—inhabiting time as participants and outside it as commentators—and epistemological—uninformed as participants and more informed as commentators.

When utilized in reality chick TV that features the tales of antiheroinist women, such as *The Real Housewives* franchise and *Sister Wives*, both discussed in subsequent chapters, the confessional serves as an intradiegetic device that delays temporal progression and bears the potential to inject feminist resistance to the text as a whole. Both *The Real Housewives* franchise and *Sister Wives*, each a docusoap that focuses on women along the various antiheroinist continua, the former composed of groups of affluent friends in various US cities and the latter of sister wives of one polygamist family, include dramatic confessionals that shed light on each show's characters. By introducing the informed subject partaking in narration in the confessional into the narrative of the uninformed object of narration whose story is enacted, the confessional opens the possibility to resist social and televisual scripts. Of course, reality narratives are often dictated by production, and confessionals are led by scripts and interviewers. Nevertheless, on the textual level, confessionals create an opportunity for resistance as do other intradiegetic devices.

The reality confessional thus works both as a narrative unit that is temporally separate from the plot—in the sense that it stands beyond the flow of each season's story arc—and as a characterization device that may shape antiheroinist resistance and subjectivity. For example, in the eleventh episode of *The Real Housewives of New Jersey*'s fourth season, cast member Teresa is accompanying her eleven-year-old daughter to a dance audition; this is depicted as a confessional in which she is commenting on the audition and is inter-edited into the audition scene. While images of her daughter Gia's audition are presented, Teresa's words in the confessional frame her daughter's performative efforts: "the world could be crumbling down," Teresa says; "I always have a smile on my face." Though Teresa is talking about herself, her words in the confessional are uttered in voice-over while Gia is dancing, thus pointing at the fact that Gia is now being socialized into smiling through hardship, maintaining composure despite circumstances, that is, performing proper femininity. The intradiegetic confessional injects the social expectation to conform to gender demands into the narrative, as if Gia is auditioning for her entrance into femininity. When crosscut against the images of a girl dancing, the intradiegetic message exposes the constructedness of feminine performance.

Arguably, executives at Bravo, the network that produces and airs *The Real Housewives*, have openly testified to utilizing ironic tones in the juxtaposition between narrative and confessionals. A chief executive has explained, "we do something with the editing that's called a Bravo wink. We wink at the audience when someone says 'I'm the healthiest person in the world' and then you see them ashing their cigarette" (Brand 2009). However, while ironic juxtaposition is often a manufactured gap in *The Real Housewives*, the potential for textual resistance is still embedded in the intradiegetic intervention of the confessional. The mise-en-scène of Gia's dance, crosscut with Teresa's confessional, may present an ironic wink designed to spotlight a woman unaware of her conduct. Read against the narrative it delays, however, the intradiegetic confessional exposes the constructedness of the binds of feminine performance. Thus, though the scene follows an entertaining audition, the confessional restructures its message.

Intradiegetic devices that delay the narrative progression appear in many forms and in many genres, including such that focus on men's characters. As the following chapters demonstrate, many of the temporal features analyzed in this book are not solely related to women's texts but are found in many texts, especially those of contemporary US television series. Nevertheless, I argue that when such appear in chick TV texts, temporal complexity's resistance to narrative order also resists patriarchal order. When temporal delay occurs in men-driven texts, it does not signify a departure from patriarchal values but, instead, overlooks them, maintains them, or reinforces them. *Lost* (2004–10) is a dominant example of a text in which the many temporal departures work to strengthen masculine performance rather than challenge it (Magill 2011) and mostly contribute to the storytelling rather than transform the narrative order. Correspondingly, *Mad Men*'s offerings of departures from narrative temporal order are textualized as allegories of the main narrative or the series' historical contexts (see, for example, Rustad and Vermeulen [2012] on "the pear scene"), and *Supernatural*'s blurring of past and present is used to immerse viewers in the story and signify the perpetuation of the past constantly haunting the present (Fuchs 2012). These examples indicate that temporal complexities in men-driven narratives work mostly to affirm, develop, and deepen narrative order rather than resist it.

Intradiegetic resistance is revealed through textual reading—to reveal the resistances offered by these devices, one must read their intradiegetic work against the diegesis. If intradiegetic devices that delay the temporal flow of chick TV series offer a feminist resistance that is covert in the text, it bears asking: what happens to the feminist politics of temporality and antiheroinism in more overt instances of temporal delay or disruption? Chapter 2 addresses antiheroinist feminist resistance in temporal forms that are explicit in the text—temporal constructs such as flashback, flashforward, and flash-sideways.

2
Deviation

The textual devices discussed in chapter 1 subtextually delay hegemonic temporality and resist hegemonic culture by favoring women's culture and thus reveal antiheroinism through textual reading. Conversely, the temporal constructs in this chapter are such that explicitly resist hegemonic temporality and culture by deviating from chrononormativity and purposely opting out of patriarchal demands toward women. The following instances of flashbacks, flashforwards, and flash-sideways (henceforth addressed as temporal flashes) identify antiheroinism that is written into the plot, explicated via temporal play, as opposed to the previous chapter's antiheroinism, which is concealed in the text and revealed through the analysis of temporal play.

This chapter focuses on *Grey's Anatomy*, setting it in comparison to other series that present episodic temporal play, such as *Desperate Housewives* and *Six Feet Under*, and strives to ascertain the link between textual temporal complexity and antiheroinism. The three temporal flashes studied in this chapter—flashback, flashforward, and flash-sideways—all illustrate a form of delay, as all pause narrative progression for the sake of a temporal deviation, be it backward, sideways, or forward.

Grey's Anatomy: Deviating from the Hegemonic Flow

Grey's Anatomy chronicles the goings-on at a Seattle hospital, including the work dynamics and interpersonal relationships of surgical interns, residents, and attending physicians. The series is chick TV due to its soap-operatic focus on emotion, gender, and dialogue, and its emphasis on women characters, women's subjectivity, and feminine performance (looking at family, relationships, friendships, sex, and work). Often dealing with illness, *Grey's Anatomy* foregrounds stories with an "emphasis on the here, the present, the now" as a result of the rejection of a future endangered by maladies. According to Halberstam, "while the threat of no future hovers overhead like a storm cloud, the urgency of being also expands the potential of the moment and . . . squeezes new possibilities out of the time at hand" (2005, 2).[1] *Grey's Anatomy* is an example of a text that continuously challenges social certainties about what constitutes the "right" time, duration, or frequency of social practices. The series often introduces characters who resist normative life choices, specifically women who stray from the antiheroinist continua's midpoints regarding family, domesticity, sex, propriety, etc., with breaks and swerves from chrononormative order.

One notable example of the way in which the series works to challenge both social and narrative expectation regarding time and the performance of femininity is the resistance of a woman with an inoperable tumor to abide by the romantic notions of the medical staff members who try to persuade her to undergo futile surgery so as to earn herself, and perhaps even more so the staff, the opportunity to imagine a future. *Grey's Anatomy* nevertheless resists the temptation to offer a happy ending to the patient's narrative and, instead of presenting a miracle, concludes the episode with a final note by which the patient maintains her present-favoring ethos, distanced from social conventions. When the cardiovascular surgeon comes in with a new surgical plan, telling the patient she could give her her life back, the patient says "yes, but this is my life, I don't need it back. I don't need the white picket fence and the bunch of kids and dogs crawling over me, or whatever kind of future you think you could give me because you can't.

---

1. This quote is taken from a paragraph in which Halberstam addresses the temporality of dealing with AIDS, by which there is a "diminishing future" and, as a result, a thickening present (2005).

I don't need a future. I have exactly what I want right now" (*Grey's Anatomy*, season 13, episode 22, "Leave It Inside"). What this patient wants is mostly related to having casual sex and having no romantic or familial commitment. This example, closely resembling Halberstam's emphasis on the present (2005), reflects the ethos of the series, which often calls into question normative conceptions of time.[2]

In the tradition of medical dramas, *Grey's Anatomy* seems to be maintaining a fairly conventional structure. Not unlike its predecessors, such as *St. Elsewhere* (1982–88), *Chicago Hope* (1994–2000), or *ER* (1994–2009), *Grey's Anatomy* works under a soap-opera-like form, with an ensemble cast of which many are dominant and occupying the center of episodes (usually every episode focuses on the storyline of a few characters of the ensemble, with not all gaining the same amount of attention), a continual story arc throughout seasons (single-episode storylines weaved into seasonal arcs), and a continuous, mostly causal, temporal progression devoid of time swerves. However, *Grey's Anatomy* occasionally introduces "breaks in narrative time flow" (Booth 2012, 195) with instances that bring forth a play with temporality that is not common to the genre's predominantly realistic mode. Another exception in the medical drama genre is *Nurse Jackie*, which incorporates temporal play, primarily intradiegetic, as illustrated in chapter 1.[3] The temporal play in *Grey's Anatomy* is more explicit, evinced in temporal flashes—flashback, flash-sideways, and flashforward.

---

2. Though conformity with normativity is pursued in *Grey's Anatomy* in myriad ways, the series also often allows for normativity to be questioned.

3. *ER*'s episode "Ambush" (season 4, episode 1) is a paradigmatic exception as it depicts a live-like documentary-style temporality as the episode is unfolded through the lens of a diegetic film crew. The live-like temporality deviates from conventional fictional temporal progression as it emphasizes a present tense. Nevertheless, the episode runs linearly and realistically (one may argue that the documentary style is very much consistent with the genre's realistic tendencies in its hyperrealistic aesthetic mode) and is not indicative of the series' dominant style. Joseph Turow also mentions the realist tendencies of medical dramas and that "*Mental*, . . . the one show that explicitly went out of its way to disagree with this take on reality . . . didn't last" (2010, 387).

Flashes and Antiheroinism: The Feminist Politics of Temporal Deviation

Flashback

Flashback is one of the most common forms of temporal play, especially in visual arts (Turim 1989). Researchers observe that the flashback has become a dominant part of the narrative structure of twenty-first-century television (Booth 2012). This trope is correspondingly common in television and has become more common with the advancement of technology and the growing sophistication of storytelling techniques (Booth 2011 and 2012). Twenty-first-century television in the United States is rife with examples of flashbacks (Ames 2012; Booth 2011 and 2012; Clarke 2013; Kelly 2017; Mittell 2006 and 2015a), many of which are merely informative and some of which work to enhance characterization. In my investigation of the flashback, I focus on its effect on characterization in a manner that exceeds filling gaps in the plot as I tie chick TV flashbacks with antiheroinism. Namely, I explore flashbacks in terms of their ability "to convey female subjectivity" (Turim 1989, 75), thereby allowing for antiheroinist resistance to feminine performance in their resistance to the narrative's temporal progression.[4] So common is the flashback that it appears in nearly all twenty-first-century chick TV series, as part of memory or storytelling, including *Girls*' season 1, episode 5 ("Hard Being Easy"); *Nurse Jackie*'s season 4, episode 1 ("Kettle-Kettle-Black-Black"); and emerging every so often in *Desperate Housewives*, *Six Feet Under*, and *Grey's Anatomy*.

The *Grey's Anatomy* episode "Only Mama Knows" (season 11, episode 4) is rife with flashbacks and repeatedly circles across several

---

4. For that matter, series that utilize flashback as a plot-advancing technique are not studied here. *Orange Is the New Black*, for example, uses the flashback as a regular mechanism that unfolds the backstory of each character (Hohenstein and Thalmann 2019) to advance the plot rather than resist it and is therefore excluded from my inquiry of the form.

layers of "pasts." The episode opens with Ellis Grey, the mother of lead character Meredith Grey, as Ellis is speaking at what will later be clarified to be a ceremony where she receives an award for her medical work. Following a short medical explanation in which Ellis is shot in a close-up, the frame zooms out to reveal that the scene is in fact a recording of her playing on a screen as her daughter Meredith is watching the recording. The episode thus opens with layered temporality and focalization as the text initially focuses on Ellis and her speech but then reveals that her daughter Meredith is the main character in the scene—her voice-over narrates the scene, and her hand is in hold of the remote control that can pause, repeat, fast-forward, or rewind her mother's speech.[5]

"I was the only woman in my surgical residency program," one of Ellis's first sentences in the recording notes after the screen is uncovered and exposes the fact that the image is recorded but before Meredith's image is revealed to be watching the recording. "They called me 'the girl' and 'Mrs. Grey,'" Ellis adds, at which point Meredith's face is revealed as she smirks knowingly, perhaps identifying with her mother's experience with sexism or possibly sneering at the blunt version of previous generations' prejudices. "Along with the one Black male resident," Ellis continues, "I was clearly excluded. They didn't want me to be a part of their boys' club. So I did the only audacious thing you can do with an audacious technique; I got myself published in the *Journal of American Medicine*." At this point, the text abandons the recording and returns to the observer's temporal realm as the frame presents Meredith's spouse entering the room, appearing disapproving. Meredith does not pause the recording, however, and stares back at her husband with resentment. He leaves the room, and the recording of Ellis persists, voicing "that caused an uproar; a resident was not first author of a published paper. But the truly audacious part came when they saw what I named my technique—'The Grey

---

5. The turn to the past is, in this case, mediated by video, unlike other shifts backward, such as flashbacks that follow the memories of characters or flashbacks that conjure scenes from earlier seasons.

Method.' I put my own name on it. You should have heard the boys roar about that."

The episode thus opens with both a connection to the past—the recording of Meredith's mother, who at the point of the diegetic present is deceased—and explicit resistance to patriarchal oppression—Ellis insists on her agency in the face of patriarchal oppression. The video—a remnant from the past—triggers the dual function of the flashback articulated by Maureen Turim: to explore the inner thoughts of a character, in this case Meredith, and the "psychoanalytical constructs of the narrative" (1989, 78), in this case, notions of memory, history, and feminine performance.[6] In "Only Mama Knows," the link between leaps into the past and antiheroinist feminist resistance sets the tone of the episode. This expository scene establishes a connection between Meredith in the diegetic present and Ellis in the diegetic past. The two temporal realms are continuously intertwined throughout the episode as the women's respective antiheroinist resistances to patriarchal order, struggling with sexist perceptions and with exclusion by men coworkers and lovers, will be correlated through the episode's flashbacks.

After Ellis's anecdote, Meredith pauses the recording, and her voice-over (which usually launches each episode) utters

> This is how my mother wanted to be remembered. My memory of her is a little bit different. . . . I'm sure everyone remembers their own version of her. Versions I wouldn't even recognize. It's all that's really left of someone when they're gone. No . . . but that's the tricky thing. Nobody's memory is perfect or complete. . . . We jumble things up. We lose track of time. We are in one place and another, and it all feels like one long, inescapable moment. It's just like my mother used to say—the carousel never stops turning.[7]

---

6. The character of Ellis Grey died in season 3 (episode 17, "Some Kind of Miracle") but returned as a figure of recollection and in flashbacks several times after that.

7. Parts of this monologue, including flashback images and the carousel motif, repeat later in the season (at which point with images from "Only Mama Knows" as well), creating ripples of repetition for the jumps in temporality.

This voice-over track accompanies a montage of various flashbacks, mixing scenes that were parts of previous episodes with scenes that were not, of both Meredith and Ellis at different ages and "pasts." Memory and (diegetic) history are tangled as flashbacks representing Meredith's subjective memory are interwoven with flashbacks that unfold the pasts of the series' characters, the latter recounted as diegetic "history" and devoid of characters' point of view.

This amalgamation of Meredith's subjective memory of her mother with flashbacks that repeat scenes of her mother previously aired situates both Grey women as struggling to position themselves between prescribed identity and subjectivity (Seel 2006). In the episode's present, Meredith is arguing with her spouse Derek over the sacrifices they each made regarding their family and careers. Meredith's main argument with her spouse in this episode is about being free to take her time, literally. Seeing as he let go of a job opportunity so she could keep her job, she feels obligated to justify his decision. "You want to hear that I cured cancer or that I found a vaccine for ALS before breakfast," she tells him, stressing,

> You're waiting for me to pay up for this grand sacrifice that you made for our family. How am I supposed to do anything with you pressuring me and hovering over me for a decision that you made? And you're waiting for me to fail. . . . It was you who decided to stay here and martyr yourself and now make me feel guilty because of a decision you made.

Meredith thus does not want to shine or fail; she just wants to "have her time." When her husband retorts, following her monologue, that she sounds like her mother, she responds: "You could do worse than compare me to a brilliant surgeon, but you meant it in the sense that I am cold and ambitious and selfish, a horrible wife and mother." Cold, ambitious, and selfish here signify antiheroinist resistance to the expectation that women be selfless nurturers, comparing Ellis's determination not to sacrifice her profession for family with Meredith's similar aspirations. The flashbacks thus continuously link antiheroinist resistance between generations (the two women's surgical successes are crosscut, the carousel leitmotif systematically returns throughout the episode, the daughter reads her dead mother's journals). More so than her mother, however, Meredith not only resists the patriarchal expectation to prioritize romantic and familial obligations but also resists the capitalistic expectation to excel. She longs to deviate from the social order (not fail or shine). The flashback, a deviation from narrative order, bestows Meredith with a deviation from patriarchal order.

The flashback serves as a bridge between present and past, a juncture that connects Ellis and Meredith through the ages, thus constructing a temporal space through which Meredith finds agency. The past plays a crucial role in the present, via flashbacks, not only as its lesson but also as its potential transformer. A rereading of the past may shift the politics of the present—a reconsideration of Ellis's legacy shifts the course of Meredith's life choices. By tapping into the archive of her mother's struggles—by video, journals, and memories—Meredith realizes she needs a break from social expectations. The flashbacks antiheroinize Meredith along the sexual and domestic continua as they propel her to risk her romantic and familial stability.

As "Only Mama Knows" shifts back and forth between several temporal frames, it presents a text in which lies a channel of what Hélène Cixous terms "open memory," by which woman holds memory as part of accepting it rather than withholding it. Open memory in a sense keeps an open pathway between past and present as it "ceaselessly makes way" (Cixous 1981, 54). By means of the open channel between past and present via memory in "Only Mama Knows," the text absorbs Ellis's and Meredith's experiences and, by way of comparison, antiheroinizes both along the domestic and intellectual continua—resisting their roles as nurturers and insisting on their intellectual capabilities. The textual open memory reveals the resistant forces in each of the women. Turim relates to a form of "working-class biographies," in which narration is unfolded through flashbacks that are "focalized by the anti-hero or anti-heroine as suits a confession. . . . The working-class anti-hero or anti-heroine [may] gain a knowledge of self that provides the means to continue or even change" (Turim 1989, 122). The flashbacks in "Only Mama Knows" similarly prompt Meredith to "gain a knowledge of self," focusing on her antiheroinist self, which insists on challenging existing order and effecting change.

The temporal circularity produced by the flashbacks in "Only Mama Knows" is reflected in the eleventh episode of the fourteenth season titled "(Don't Fear) the Reaper," in which Miranda Bailey is the episode protagonist. This episode also merges flashbacks from Miranda's past (childhood, teenage years, early adulthood) that were never seen in the series with flashbacks from her past before the series started but which were already featured in the text (namely, that when initially featured, they were already framed as flashbacks) and with flashbacks from earlier seasons that were the diegetic present when first aired. "(Don't Fear) the Reaper" likewise springs between mother and daughter (Miranda and her mother) in a range of timeframes, as well as between various instances in Miranda's life with her husband, friends, and coworkers. Further analogously to "Only Mama Knows," the flashbacks in "(Don't Fear) the Reaper" work to characterize Miranda and her form of motherhood and daughterhood vis-à-vis notions of sacrifice, women's health, and gender-oriented and race-oriented silencing and dismissal.

Being a Black woman, Miranda occupies an antiheroinism that is racialized and not just gendered, as her complex characterization stands in constant tension with conservative characterizations that are not only sexist but also racist. While white women's representation usually divides between two extremes—either the Madonna or the whore—the representation of Black women also includes the Sapphire image: "The image of the hostile, nagging Black woman . . . personified by the character Sapphire on the 1940s and 1950s Amos 'n' Andy radio and television shows." Traces of the Sapphire character can be found "in many cultural texts" (West 2012, 296), from the "bitch," to the "sassy" friend, and the "angry Black woman."

Whereas all women's misconduct is often dismissed as "bitchy" rather than antiheroic, women of color who sidestep propriety are at higher risk of stereotypization and are subjected to both sexist and racist vilification, both diegetically and extradiegetically. An infamous example of extradiegetic criticism against Miranda as an "angry Black woman" can be seen in Alessandra Stanley's 2014 *New York Times* column in which she argued that many of the characters in the shows of *Grey's Anatomy* creator Shonda Rhimes, including Miranda, are reflections of "an angry Black woman."[8] According to Carolyn West, the dismissal of Black women as angry rather than complex through misogynistic and racist stereotypization "implies that Black women's anger, their justifiable response to societal injustice, is dangerous or funny" (2012, 296). By reducing complex and resistant (that is, antiheroinist) Black women characters to a racial stereotype, hegemonic culture pathologizes their often-justifiable anger, thereby perpetuating their marginalization and belittlement.

This devaluation of resistant Black women as unjustifiably disposed to anger, regardless of how justifiable their resistance may be, resonates in *Grey's Anatomy*'s diegesis as well. "(Don't Fear) the Reaper" exposes the same mechanism by which Black women are dismissed as "angry" as Miranda's legitimate appeals for medical care are disregarded as excessive. In the episode, Miranda arrives at a hospital (different from the one in which she is employed as chief of surgery) insisting she is undergoing a heart attack. Because she is not exhibiting symptoms usually identified as a heart attack, the medical staff is convinced that her problem is psychiatric and not physical. When Miranda realizes her condition has not been taken seriously and a psychiatrist was sent to see her and not a cardiovascular specialist, she tells the psychiatrist, "63 percent of women who die suddenly from coronary heart disease had no previous symptoms, and women of color are at a far greater risk." It is later revealed that Miranda was indeed having a heart attack with gender and racial bias behind the dismissal of her complaints as "hysterical" rather than the valid reports of physical pain they turned out to be.

---

8. Stanley's column provoked numerous media responses that slammed the piece as racist and tone-deaf.

"(Don't Fear) the Reaper" reveals the mechanism by which Black women who break decorum are discredited and snubbed as nagging hostile "Sapphires." The episode is filled with flashbacks from different eras of Miranda's life, childhood memories, giving birth to her son, her wedding, and more, as if her entire life is flashing before the viewers' eyes. However, instead of functioning as a summary of her life and a foreshadowing of her death, the flashbacks work to antiheroinize Miranda, reconstructing her characterization. The following episode (season 14, episode 12, "Harder, Better, Faster, Stronger") finds Miranda resting after her heart procedure (she is known to work continuously regardless of circumstances) as well as pursuing new research about which she is passionate. While it seems that her heart attack may be the reason for Miranda's new take on life, reading her characterization vis-à-vis flashbacks divulges their impact on her antiheroinization. Among the wide-ranging flashbacks in "(Don't Fear) the Reaper," flashbacks that center on Miranda's relationship with her mother across different ages consistently return. In these flashbacks, Miranda's overprotective mother tries to prevent Miranda from taking risks. Even though she is not as cautious as her mother encourages her to be—to her mother's dismay, she stays out reading after dark as a child or goes off to college as a young woman—the hardworking, successful Miranda has maintained fairly conservative professional choices as a surgeon and as a manager. Following many flashbacks inserted into her story, however, the oft-perceived realistic, dependable, and strict Miranda opts for a creative and audacious medical invention. With the flashbacks' deviation from narrative order, Miranda deviates from social order in her resistance along the intellectual continuum as she dares to insist on her knowledge and professionalism despite attempts to oppress them.

The dismissal of complex resistant women characters as "bitches" or "hysterics"—rather than labeling them antiheroines—is complicated further in the case of resistant women of color, as they must endure both gender and racial disparagement to be valued as antiheroines. The flashbacks in "(Don't Fear) the Reaper," as in "Only Mama Knows," work to position Miranda vis-à-vis issues of performance of femininity as well as her struggle with and resistance to prescribed social, racial, and gender identities. In both episodes, the flashbacks work to characterize Meredith and Miranda's antiheroinism, basing antiheroinism as tied with time. Certainly, *Grey's Anatomy* features flashbacks that serve the subject position of men, such as the episode "Danger Zone" (season 14, episode 5), which focalizes the flashbacks of Owen Hunt, the episode "Old Scars, Future Hearts" (season 14, episode 15), in which several flashbacks are presented, including some to the childhood of Alex Karev, or the episode "Love of My Life" (season 16, episode 19), in which flashbacks add details to the biography of Cormac Hayes. Nevertheless, the flashbacks that accompany the storylines of men are mostly such that step outside temporal progression only to fill plot-related gaps and return to progression. These are flashbacks that Anna Powell (2007) marks as those that "confirm the narrative's linear progression" rather than flashbacks that offer a destabilization of the narrative's temporality, engendering "a fragmentation of all linearity" (Powell 2007, 39, also quoting Deleuze 1989). While for Cormac, Owen, and Alex, the flashbacks fill gaps in plot and reinforce existing characteristics, for Miranda and Meredith, the flashbacks are reconstructing and antiheroinizing.

A form of the flashback also appears in nonscripted texts, including the chick TV form of the women-centered docusoap. Though reality television cannot focalize flashbacks to seem like memories of a specific cast member, it often uses previously aired footage to compare episodes' diegetic present with past scenes. These "textual flashbacks" are frequently integrated during confessionals to contrast a character's confession with her or his behavior in earlier representations (Lee and Moscowitz 2013) or during reunion episodes, in which the show's participants gather to revisit the events of the season. As part of a reunion episode, usually monitored by a host, clips of the season's highlights are integrated as triggers for discussion, sparking conflict and enflaming old disputes. Pier Dominguez discusses the complex temporality of *The Real Housewives*' reunions as women relive past events through recordings and comment retrospectively as if in the present. According to Dominguez, "the chronologies of filming and airing are reconciled and further confused through the reunion, in which the women get to comment on their feelings about what they have witnessed throughout the season in a talk show setting" (2015, 166).

While chronologies are reconciled and confused, reunions are highly formulated, with the incorporation of past events controlled by production to incite specific conflicts, ostensibly approaching toward resolution but constantly working to reignite conflict (Dominguez 2015, 167). Whereas docusoap's utilization of intradiegetic temporal delay reframes the narrative (as elaborated in chapter 1), its more explicit use of temporal play, as in the case of flashbacks, usually works to "confirm the narrative's linear progression" (Powell 2007, 39), in filling narrative gaps, ironically commenting on characters, or reigniting old conflicts. Following analyses of flashforward and flash-sideways in the next sections, chapter 3, "Serialization," addresses the transformative power of serial ties between ostensibly conservative episodes of chick TV, focusing on the formulaic *Real Housewives*. Scripted chick TV flashbacks often work to reconstruct temporality and antiheroinize women characters, as is the case with flashforwards and flash-sideways.

Flashforward

Like the flashback, the flashforward has grown increasingly prevalent in twenty-first-century television (Ames 2012; Booth 2012). Often spreading out alternative futures and imaginable times to come, the flashforward is used as an instrument that sheds light on characters' possible developments, thereby commenting on their social performance and introspectiveness.[9] Unlike many other forms of temporal

---

9. As the early twenty-first century introduced heavy temporal play, including leaps into the future, the mid-2010s featured numerous futuristic dystopian series that do not leap into the future but exist within it. Such dystopian visions include *The Leftovers* (2014–17), *Into the Badlands* (2015–19), *Westworld* (2016–), *Incorporated* (2016–17), *The Handmaid's Tale* (2017–), *Dystopia* (2019–), and others, taking up on the trend of episodic temporal play and implementing it on the arc of

play, the flashforward does not slow (slow-motion/repetition), stop (freeze, displacement), or set back (flashback, reverse) the chrononormative "time of history," which represents hegemonic masculinity (Kristeva 1981) but, rather, accelerates it, skips it, or runs through it. Nevertheless, the flashforward delays the linear progression of the temporal flow of narrative as it shifts to a different—future—temporal frame. Though the progression of time from which the deviations veer proceeds forward, the case of flashforward consists of an accelerated drive forward, elapsing the time of the story and leaping forward into the future with a cut from the narrative frame. The form of resistance the flashforward embraces lies in its capacity to offer an alternative to chrononormativity, to construct a more meandering, indirect movement of time, which defies linearity by shifting from it and deviating from its straightness.

The utilization of the flashforward technique allows the chick TV woman character "to enter into her own 'future'" (Swanson 1981, 83), thereby envisioning her own existence rather than following the one that is dictated to her by society. Thus, though drawn to a future, the flashforward does not necessarily validate the hegemonic rush to the future of "the time of history" (Kristeva 1981, 17). Indeed, despite its future-bound positioning, the flashforward deviates from chrononormativity, first, because it diverges from its prescribed pace and, second, because it opens the possibility to imagine an alternative future. Thus, entering into one's own future emphasizes one's articulation of one's future in place of the future dictated by chrononormativity, thus bearing the potential to challenge social scripts about the "right" time, duration, or frequency of social practices. In what follows, I look at the flashforward that occupies the majority of the seventeenth episode of *Grey's Anatomy* tenth season, to be later measured against leaps into the future as they appear in *Six Feet Under* and *Girls* and equating them with the ellipsis featured in *Desperate Housewives*.

---

an entire series. It remains to be seen at the time of writing how the 2020 pandemic may affect forthcoming televisual visions of the future.

These analyses focus on the interplay between accelerated movement forward in time with antiheroinism.

The flashforward has the power to antiheroinize as it resists textual and temporal order in a way that can resist the social order. An emblematic example of a flashforward that opens up a woman's alternative future is the one laid out in *Grey's Anatomy*'s tenth season storyline of Cristina Yang's imagined futures. The episode "Do You Know?" (season 10, episode 17) delves into the character of Cristina Yang, one of the main characters in the series, as she contemplates her future. More accurately, the episode captures Cristina at a fraught juncture in her life as she is adamant about devoting her life to her career and not having children, while her partner, fellow doctor Owen Hunt, longs to be a parent. The episode follows Cristina on a dramatic day in which she is to decide whether to choose her romantic love or her professional passion and unfolds two possible futures for her.

In the first future the episode presents, Cristina is happily childless and professionally and romantically satisfied. Also in this future, however, the man she loves is dissatisfied by their fate of career-driven childlessness and is miserable and unfulfilled. The second future the episode depicts is one in which Owen is content in fatherhood, but Cristina is discontented, absorbed in reluctant motherhood, sacrificing her professional passion for romantic and domestic pursuits. For Cristina, staying with Owen thus means happiness for one and inevitable misery for the other, as having children is key for Owen's sense of self and not having children is key for Cristina's.

"Do You Know?" opens with Cristina's voice-over narration, framing the episode's relationship with time and antiheroinism:

> Do you know who you are? Do you know what's happened to you? Do you want to live this way? All it takes is one person, one patient, one moment to change your life forever. It can change your perspective, color your thinking. One moment that forces you to re-evaluate everything you think you know. Do you know who you are? Do you know what's happened to you? Do you want to live this

way? Do you know who you are? Do you know what's happened to you? Do you want to live this way?[10]

Addressing both issues of identity ("do you know who you are?") and temporality ("do you know what's happened?" and "one moment that forces you to evaluate"), the opening voice-over establishes both the episode's forthcoming temporal play, manifest in the twofold flashforward, and its antiheroinist characterization, expressed in Cristina's calling of social scripts into question. After uttering "do you want to live this way," Cristina stares straight into the camera, both setting her image as the focal point of the episode and defying her role as looked-at, asserting herself as subject and refusing to be only an object.

Concluding the cold open is an encounter between Cristina and Owen, whom she proclaims is "the love of my life," and to whom she confesses she feels they must resolve their conflicts and be together. The remainder of the episode focuses on the couple's unresolvable conflicts, jumping back and forth between the present and the two opposing future timelines. The episode sees Cristina pregnant and anxious in one future, passionately pursuing research in the other, immersed in exhausting parenting in one, winning awards in the other. By the end of the episode, Cristina is forced to decide whether to get back with Owen, achieving love but also frustration, or to let go of their romance, choosing professional fulfillment. The episode emphasizes that Cristina's eventual decision, to give up her relationship, is influenced by knowledge gained via flashforward.

Thus, the flashforward helps Cristina make decisions regarding her present relationship and career, as if the text retains the memory of the flashforward. Initially, Cristina's characterization in the series is

---

10. That sequence of questions repeats later in the episode, both as voice-over commentary on the character's introspection and as part of the plot, when attempting to assess a postop patient's orientation. When delivered as voice-over commentary, the utterance, which in itself contains repetition, is often accompanied by temporal play, including slow-motion, reversal, and, of course, flashforward.

somewhat antiheroinist, as she resists feminine performance by being consciously cold and competitive (rather than nurturing and empathetic), puts herself first, rejects motherhood, and continuously struggles against the performances expected of her as a woman. Addressing the characterization of Cristina Yang, Latham Hunter asserts that she "is faced with self-sacrificing models of womanhood that are at odds with her own sensibilities" (2008, 95); Lisa Knisely notes that "she is depicted as coolly rational, cuttingly ironic, and decidedly unemotional and unaffectionate," adding that this "depiction of femininity found in Cristina's character inverts traditional ideas about masculinity and femininity" (2008, 124); and Barbara Biederer states that her unaffectedness and attention to work over sentiment "deliberately counterpoints the stereotypical emotional response so often ascribed to women" (2016, 7). Cristina thus resists along all antiheroinist continua, a characterization further complicated via the antiheroinization of the flashforward.

Moreover, her character, an Asian American, deals with a double social marginalization, both as a woman and as part of an ethnic minority, with the latter category having its own set of socially prescribed identities that may conflict with her personal experiences as subject. Belonging thus to an ethnic minority within a gender minority, Cristina is positioned as an antiheroine who attempts to resist hegemonic time and culture in more ways than one.[11] Beyond her initial inclination for antiheroinist characterization, however,

---

11. *Grey's Anatomy* has been criticized (and sometimes lauded) for presenting a postfeminist, postracial fantasy world in which inequalities do not exist (Warner 2014; Levine 2013). Although the series tackles sexual, racial, and gender-based discrimination, it arguably confronts sexism more than it does racism. Moreover, as the seasons progressed and more racial issues were narrativized, the institutional discrimination and targeting of African Americans were usually in focus (as in the case of police violence against Black individuals and communities in the episode "Personal Jesus" in season 14, episode 10), and other minorities' conflicts with stereotypes and experiences with racism, including those of Asian American Cristina, seldom get center stage.

the flashforward in "Do You Know?" further antiheroinizes her as it pushes her to reimagine a future that favors her subjectivity over prescribed identity. Instead of opting for the romantic happy ending, to which narrative order usually aspires, "Do You Know?" breaks the chrononormative flow by offering a flashforward of a less romantic view of the post-happy-ending existence. The flashforward delays temporal progression and allows Cristina to choose differently from the future to which she is expected to aspire. Indeed she does. She chooses to relinquish the happy ending, let go of her romantic aspirations, and favor her professional aspirations.

Though "Do You Know?" ends with Cristina's decision to choose career over love, later episodes show the decision is not that final. However, the departure of actress Sandra Oh (who plays Cristina) at the end of the tenth season (seven episodes after the flashforward narrative) forced a choice into the text. In correspondence with Cristina's characterization, reinforced by the "Do You Know?" flashforward, the series culminates Cristina's storyline with her leaving to pursue a job overseas while her loved one stays behind (season 10, episode 24, "Fear (Of the Unknown)"). Through the flashforward, the text antiheroinizes her into imagining a chrono-resistant future, thereby reconstructing her present and, with it, narrative and patriarchal order.

Significantly, "Do you Know?" marks the shifts in temporality through no other visual signifiers than a fade-to-white. Viewers therefore may miss the fact that the episode unfolds possible futures and perceive the occurrences as present tense until a return back in time marks the leap to the future as temporal excess. No dream-like lens manipulation, color play, or partial blurring of the frame signify the flashforward, only a gradual change in scrub-style and cellular phone design. The lack of visual difference may signify the text's effort to insert the future into the present, positioning it as part of the story rather than as excess and pointing to the divergence in Cristina's future as inherent to her character rather than as external circumstances. The flashforward, an explicit form of temporal play, is part of Cristina's characterization, antiheroinizing her.

Moreover, a secondary plotline of the episode follows Cristina's two futures—one in which a terminally ill patient opts for life-sustaining measures and the other in which the patient chooses to cease life support. As part of the narrative branch in which the patient continues to live, his wife discusses her shift from "wife" to "nursemaid and a cook and an orderly" as she takes care of her debilitated spouse.[12] The secondary plotline reflects the episode's focus on women's "prescribed identity" (Seel 2006) as constructed by wifely duties consisting of servitude and sacrifice. Cristina's resistance to the sacrificial demands of womanhood in general and motherhood in particular marks her feminist resistance to hegemonic ideology regarding gender, thus marking her antiheroinism. Consequently, the leaps into the future work as instruments of characterization—in Cristina's case, that of antiheroinization—thereby tying together the resistance offered by temporal play and antiheroinism.

The flashforward in *Grey's Anatomy* is an instrument of antiheroinism as the work of the complex temporality of the flash is also a work of complex characterization; the resistance to chrononormativity is resistance to gender expectations. The flashforward as antiheroinization can be seen in other chick TV texts which design the leap forward in ways that work to antiheroinize women characters. For example, *Six Feet Under* presents a multilayered and lengthy flashforward that concludes the series finale ("Everyone's Waiting," season 5, episode 12). The flashforward in the series finale portrays Claire, one of the main characters in the series, as she is driving from Los Angeles to New York, with scenes depicting the deaths of each of the series' main characters interweaved into the driving sequence. Claire, roughly twenty years old by the final season, exhibits antiheroinist characteristics throughout the series, as she constantly reconsiders her position on matters of feminine performance, from appearance to

12. "And I never go home from that work; I am that work; that's all I am anymore," she continues. Following her heartfelt confession, the patient's wife apologizes for being "selfish and horrible," stressing that her difficulty with her assigned role as caretaker is not proper.

family to her struggle with the role of caregiver to her sexual identity. Writing about Claire's character, Janet McCabe articulates that she is constantly "out to debunk clichés defining normative feminine roles while changing the script in the process" (2005, 128).

Throughout the future-death-scenes sequence, the *Six Feet Under* final episode crosscuts two temporal dimensions—the vicenarian Claire driving on a desert road and the many future death scenes, each taking place at a different time in the diegetic future. In many of those death scenes, Claire herself is seen as she is getting older, until the final death scene depicts her own death at the age of 102 as she is lying in bed with the camera surveying her bedroom and focusing on pictures hung on her walls. The pictures present both instances that were featured in episodes of the series and images of events that are set to have unfolded sometime between Claire's drive east and her death some eighty years later. The sequence thus merges various layers of future and past—the rush forward is also very much embedded in the past.

An important difference between the *Grey's Anatomy* flashforward and that in *Six Feet Under* is that the former occurs midseries, at a point from which the characters' fates may swerve, whereas the latter marks the conclusion of the series, as a final note on the fates of the characters, a fate the text will not be able to renegotiate as the series will have terminated once the future sequence is done. Still, the *Six Feet Under* ending sequence occasionally returns to the moment with which the flashforward started for a close-up on the young Claire's face driving and, after the final death scene, that of Claire as the screen fades to white and then reveals the eyes of the young Claire again, looking sideways as if searching for something, still driving toward what is still an unknown future. By returning to the diegetic present rather than ending with the leap to the future, the text insists on the way the flashforward transforms Claire's character, revealing that the flashforward is that which allows her subjectivity in the present. Impacted by the flashforward, that is, Claire is antiheroinistically driving at her own volition toward the future she chooses. Though the playing out of the characters' deaths may seem deterministic, the flashforward insinuates that the possibility to imagine a future may work to transform it.

Between *Grey's Anatomy*'s midseries flashforward and *Six Feet Under*'s concluding flashforward, *Girls* incorporates a flashforward in the series' penultimate episode ("Goodbye Tour," season 6, episode 9). In the flashforward, the series protagonist, antiheroine Hannah Horvath, is at a party, and her impending (impending at the time of the party) move to upstate New York is crosscut against scenes from the party. The episode crosscuts Hannah dancing at the party with her driving to her new home (with aesthetics very reminiscent of Claire's driving to New York) and organizing it. Further complicating the temporality of the flashforward, the scenes after the party—those in which Hannah is driving to her new home and setting it up—are not edited chronologically. She is seen driving, then unpacking, then driving again, then sitting in her new living room. This multilayered flashforward appears neither in the middle of the series nor at its very end, but rather toward the end, leaving space to negotiate the transpiring future, but only the space of a single episode. In comparison, *Grey's Anatomy*'s flashforward is such that it heavily influences the text that follows it—in the sense that Cristina's antiheroinist life choices were affected by the flashforward as if she had truly lived it—and *Six Feet Under*'s flashforward is such that antiheroinizes only a moment, at least in the textual framework that is open to analysis, seeing as no further episodes were issued following the finale flashforward.

Thus, the amount of text that follows a flashforward defines the significance of the flashforward. In *Grey's Anatomy* it is an experience that alters the present; in *Six Feet Under* it is an endnote that concludes with tying present with future and allowing a "sense of the image of [one]self" (Swanson 1981, 83) in the present; and in *Girls* it is a parenthetical note that serves as a kairotic moment, however brief and temporary, significant in terms of characterization, as from that moment on new, fantastic possibilities that still cannot be fathomed in the diegetic present find their way into that present. Simply put, the flashforward catalyzes feminist politics in the way that it opens a possibility that resists present hegemonic axioms. The more text following the flashforward, the more the flashforward works to antiheroinize as its influence is further cemented in the text and in the character; the knowledge of the future is injected into the present, and the antiheroine's resistant force is intensified.

Interestingly, the following episode after *Girls*' "Goodbye Tour," that is, *Girls*' series finale ("Latching," season 6, episode 10), opens with a short exposition that is timed not long after the events in "Goodbye Tour," but then presents an ellipsis, skipping five months ahead. On the level of storytelling, while the flashforward functions as a movement into the future from which the text returns to the diegetic present, the ellipsis is a leap forward from which the text does not return. In the ellipsis, the future to which the text leaps becomes the new present. After the ellipsis, "Latching" shows Hannah in the house to which she moved at the end of "Goodbye Tour," but the happy-ending mode that accompanied the move is replaced with discomfort and angst. As Hannah was pregnant in "Goodbye Tour," "Latching" encounters her with her baby now born. As a result, post-flashforward Hannah's antiheroinism is related mostly to resistant motherhood rather than the resistant sexuality or sociality by which her antiheroinism was marked during the majority of the series before the flashforward. In this case, the flashforward works to change the type of her antiheroinism.

In the episode, Hannah fulfills motherhood, fundamentally a practice of preservation of order, but she does so in a manner that insists on marking itself as problematic and devoid of a rhetoric of resolution, which is in fact the ending tone of "Goodbye Tour." *Girls* creator Dunham has noted that "Goodbye Tour" "is sort of the more traditional finale, and then ['Latching'] is almost like a short-film epilogue" (Hiatt 2017). Thus, the addition of "Latching" after the resolution-like tone of the penultimate "Goodbye Tour" highlights the series' resistance to order in its insistence on ending on a note of disorder rather than order. *Girls* does not illustrate motherhood as a happy ending but as a continuous state of disequilibrium. It is as if the flashforward helped Hannah transition from resistant girlhood to resistant motherhood—to adulthood that does not need to be compliant with the social order (as she feared her adulthood would be) but can maintain a resistant aspect that is reconciled with antiheroinism.

The ellipsis in this case coacts with the flashback to position the antiheroine in a new form of antiheroinism. What, then, of ellipsis as an independent textual construct? *Desperate Housewives*, the chick TV series that follows four suburban housewives, presents an ellipsis in the move from the fourth season to the fifth as the latter starts five years after the former ends. The series combines soap narrative with dark and comic undertones, foregrounding women characters, their relationships, and families with mystery storylines. Unlike a flashforward—which sneaks a peek into the future and returns to the present armed with tools to shape that which is to come—the ellipsis in *Desperate Housewives* leaps into the future and "stays" there, thus making the future the new diegetic present. The following *Desperate Housewives* seasons after the ellipsis (the series spanned eight seasons) continue the same timeline launched by season five. *Desperate Housewives*' fourth season finale ("Free," season 4, episode 17), which culminates in the leap to the future, is in itself a tale of antiheroinism as the women protagonists all gather to protect their friend against patriarchal law by bending patriarchal law.

In the episode, Katherine Mayfair, one of the women in the neighborhood, shoots her ex-husband after years of being threatened by him. Having beaten her when married and stalked her once separated, Katherine's police officer ex-husband convinces his fellow officers that Katherine is slandering him and fabricating stories to demonize him, rendering her unable to benefit from the protection of the law. The episode ends with a collaborative effort by Katherine's women friends and neighbors to protect her, with all of them telling the police that she shot her ex-husband out of self-defense (which is in fact the truth). The episode's epilogue follows the series' lead characters five years later and shows that the women have overcome this challenge well into the future. Stylistically, the happy-ending tone of the fourth season finale features a flashforward, but when the fifth season starts, the text does not go "back" five years and, instead, continues onward, thus defining the leap into the future as an ellipsis rather than a flashforward.

If the flashforward stands for resistance to the hold of chrononormativity in its delay of progression in favor of a glimpse of what's to come and a consequent rerouting of the temporal flow, then the ellipsis would seem to lack a resistant force as it ostensibly skips forward to an already scripted future. Nevertheless, the final episode of *Desperate Housewives*' fourth season reflects what Linda Williams characterizes as a melodramatic "last minute rescue"—"a dialectic of pathos and action—a give and take of 'too late' and 'in the nick of time'" (Williams 1998, 69). The women of *Desperate Housewives* thus changed the patriarchal script at the last minute, usurping the patriarch (Katherine's long abusive ex-husband), and establishing a new reign of women who reset the tone. In that manner, the episode inverts the clasp of "the time of history" (Kristeva 1981, 17) and introduces a feminist resistance, thereby antiheroinistically changing the script. The ellipsis in *Desperate Housewives* thus jumps ahead to a changed future, which would not have happened had it not been for the antiheroinist resistance that occurred in "the nick of time" (Williams 1998, 69) at the end of the fourth season.

Arguably, in chick TV, most any leap to the future bears a resistant antiheroinist potential, whether returning to a changed present or changing the future itself. In comparison, leaps to the future play a different role in men-centered serials, such as *Lost* or *FlashForward*, in which flashforwards perform as what Roland Barthes (1977) terms "catalysers,"—filling plot gaps, playing with the possibilities of the medium (Booth 2012), or communicating with new modes of viewership and consumption (Johnson 2011). The flashforwards in *FlashForward* function as a manifestation of anxiety (Kelly 2017) and as a plot vehicle (McDuffie 2012) that foresees characters' fates and drives them to pursue or prevent their fates. The flashforwards in *Lost* reflect the preoccupation of the series with faith and fate (Himsel Burcon 2012), symbolize trauma (Mousoutzanis 2012), and function as a narrative strategy (Bennett 2012) that facilitates an understanding of the present. Highly complex, these flashforwards are usually in line with the narrative flow as well as the social order. Conversely, chick TV flashforwards operate as "cardinal functions" (Barthes 1977) that reconstruct narrative and characterization, antiheroinizing instruments that deviate from narrative temporality and patriarchal culture.

Flash-Sideways

As with the flashback and flashforward, the flash-sideways also creates a delay as the temporal sequence is paused and a parallel diegetic present is envisioned. The flash-sideways presents an alternative present, perceived as a form of temporal play that moves sideways across the present without shifting forward or backward in time but offering a parallel present that visualizes what would happen in the present if circumstances were different. Also similarly to flashbacks and flashforwards, the chick TV flash-sideways deviates from order and antiheroinizes women characters. In *Grey's Anatomy*, the episode "If/Then" (season 8, episode 13) presents an episode-long flash-sideways to a parallel present that not only reshuffles alliances, friendships, and relationships, but also changes the characterization of the women in the series' main ensemble.

The episode opens, as do most of the episodes in the series, with Meredith Grey's voice-over, this time discussing the randomness of existence, wondering, "what if one little thing I said or did could have made it all fall apart? What if I've chosen another life for myself? Or another person? We might have never found each other. What if I've been raised differently? What if my mother had never been sick? What if I've actually had a good father? What if?" ("If/Then"). After the opening voice-over monologue, Meredith gets into bed as the camera zooms in on her closing her eyes and waking up to a parallel present. The flash-sideways is thus framed as if envisaged by Meredith herself. However, though the episode closes with Meredith's voice-over as well, it does not return to the initial diegetic present, nor does it depict Meredith "waking up" from this parallel present. Here, too, as in other *Grey's Anatomy* flashes, it remains unclear whether the shift is subjective or textual, thereby influencing characters in later episodes, even if they exhibit no awareness of the effect of the flash, as the text itself absorbs the shift of the flash.

Most of the episode concentrates on the parallel present, with world alterations that are mainly technical—couples are paired up differently, several of the characters have different jobs, or a different number or gender of children. However, some of the changes are more profound as a few of the characters that viewers have come to know for eight seasons possess different ideologies and have different personalities altogether. Two lead women characters, Meredith and Cristina, both step out of antiheroinism in the flash-sideways but in opposite directions. While Meredith sways into heroism, with her resistant traits removed and her characterization more conformist, Cristina sways into villainessness as she is stripped of her identifiable traits and becomes a demonized outcast.

The two women, close friends in *Grey's Anatomy*'s diegetic present, become rivals in the flash-sideways marked by stylistic and characterizational opposites. Their differences—Meredith mostly wears pink and Cristina black, Meredith is ostensibly happily engaged and Cristina both romantically and socially isolated—define the opposite directions of their de-antiheroinization, the one heroinized and the other villainized. By flashing sideways, the episode wonders what would happen if these two women did not possess antiheroinist characteristics. Significantly, as in the flashback, the flash-sideways associates Meredith's personality with her relationship with her mother. "She wants everyone around her to be ordinary so she can be extraordinary," Meredith says about her mother in the episode, adding, "she wants everyone around her small." However, Meredith's realization regarding her mother comes late in the episode, after she had, in the parallel temporal realm, spent the better part of her life complying with her mother's wishes and conforming to social demands. It is a moment of crisis in "If/Then" (she learns that her parallel-present husband is cheating on her) that pushes her to question her social, professional, and familial roles, prompting the quoted realization about her mother.

This crisis-driven realization antiheroinizes Meredith and leads her to resist the complaisant character she has thus far possessed (in the parallel present), as she notes, regarding her mother's disparaging of others, "I'm not going to let her do it to me." In this instance, the flash-sideways nonresistant Meredith enters a state of antiheroinism, as she fights conformism under her mother's rule and tries to find her own path. Similarly, Cristina Yang is antiheroinized by the end of the episode, as her detached and hostile villainessness is complicated to reveal a more layered identity that is also characterized as empathetic and friendly. Both women's recharacterization is signified in a medical procedure that Meredith and Cristina perform together, a procedure in which they at first fail to cooperate and then complement each other. Thus, the text in fact antiheroinizes both Meredith and Cristina through their encounter—the heroine and the villainess move from animosity to cooperation and friendship, as if balancing each other toward antiheroinism, each complicating her one-dimensional extreme in the hero-villain dichotomy into a more complex antiheroinist characterization.

"If/Then," though clichéd in its culmination with everyone drawn back to their diegetic present positions as if they were destined for them, reinforces the link between temporal play and antiheroinism. Both Meredith and Cristina shift back from their flash-sideways characterization toward antiheroinism—Meredith in challenging authority and resisting order and Cristina in resisting her vilification and renegotiating her subjectivity. It seems, then, that the text itself expresses its necessity to invoke antiheroinism in its women characters in order to establish their sense of self.

Here, too, as with flashbacks and flashforwards, the changes that men characters undergo are different from those of women. Unlike Meredith, who changes from the resistant antiheroine she usually is in most *Grey's Anatomy* episodes into an unquestioning conformist in "If/Then" (and then antiheroinized at the end of the episode); or Cristina, who changes from a resistant antiheroine into a misanthropic villainess (and also re-antiheroinized); or Miranda, who changes from a resistant antiheroine into a submissive weakling (with hints of her process of re-antiheroinization at the end of the episode); or Callie, who changes from a resistant antiheroine into a heteronormative conformist (with hints of a queerified re-antiheroinization)—the men in the episode experience changes in circumstances but not characterization. Owen, for example, though not having the same romantic partner that he does in the series' present, maintains in the parallel present the same character he usually does; Alex, though exhibiting different characteristics, is revealed to be masquerading as that which he is not rather than being truly different or experiencing any character change; and Derek, though appearing as different, seems to be conducting himself in a different register (his life choices have led him to be more "dreary"), arguably not possessing a profoundly different character. Thus, the flash-sideways introduces a deviation from order that destabilizes chrononormativity and offers a process of antiheroinization for women characters. Through the flash-sideways, "If/Then" deviates from hegemonic temporality into an alternative temporal ex-territory in which narrative and social order can be challenged and renegotiated.

Though all three forms of temporal flashes—backward, forward, and sideways—offer a deviation from both temporal and social order, they differ from each other in their ties with social contexts. The flashback points at history, and, even if that history is entirely fictional in the world of the text, it posits the antiheroine subject in touch with her predecessors, as in the case of Meredith and her mother. The flashforward points inward, at the antiheroine's own subjectivity and her ability to imagine her desired future self, in polishing her agency, as in the case of Cristina's realization of her preferred life choices. The flash-sideways points at social circumstances as it isolates the antiheroine from her surroundings by implanting her in different circumstances, thereby focusing on the effect of social context on her subjectivity. Each direction of the flashes sheds light on different aspects that work to antiheroinize—flashback through history, flashforward through self, and flash-sideways through social context. Each flash thus offers a different strategy through which to resist chrononormativity. The comparison to personal or collective history of the flashback helps draw a line between traditional conservativism and its residues in the present that call for resistance. The process inward of the flashforward helps identify internalized oppression that calls for resistance. The juxtaposition against possible parallel presents of the flash-sideways helps point at contemporaneous circumstances by isolating the individual from environmental influences and resisting them.

Flashbacks, flashforwards, and flash-sideways appear, of course, in many texts, chick TV or not, and do not always stimulate antiheroism or antiheroinism. Still, I contend that non-chick TV texts tend to use flashes as instruments for revealing details about plot or character as windows to the (usually men) characters' history, psyche, or relationships with themselves and to destabilize narrative order for symbolic or storytelling purposes. In chick TV, however, the flashes-as-characterization time-shifts destabilize narrative order to destabilize social order. By examining historical (flashback), introspective (flashforward), or contextual (flash-sideways) frameworks, chick TV flashes challenge chrononormativity and patriarchal order.

The flashes visualize temporal realms that deviate from the hegemonic order and open the possibility of an alternative order. These temporal realms offer explicit feminist resistance and antiheroinization, unlike the more implicit forms of antiheroinist resistance of intradiegetic devices. If temporal play in episodes' narratives can be either implicit—revealed through textual reading—or explicit—inscribed in the text—it bears considering how it functions in the ties between episodes. How does the serial structure affect temporal play? How are complex textual temporalities, implicit or explicit, affected by the structure of seriality itself? Next, I examine the feminist politics of temporality and antiheroinism of seriality by looking at instances of antiheroinist feminist resistance in the structure of serial forms, focusing on the complex temporality of serialization.

3
Serialization

The flashes analyzed in chapter 2 explicitly deviate from hegemonic culture and serve as temporal constructs that form antiheroinism in chick TV series. In this chapter I look at the temporal structure of seriality itself, demonstrating that chick TV seriality bears the capacity to antiheroinize characters who are not necessarily antiheroinist but whose antiheroinism is identified through serial, intratextual reading.[1] Analysis of chick TV seriality may thus reveal resistant antiheroinism where it is implicit in the text and multiply it where it is explicit.

The structure of seriality is dependent on the intratextual ties between its parts—episodes and seasons—and between the parts and the whole—the series. The ties between episodes and between seasons affect the tone of the text, as, for example, the fact that the flashforward at the end of the fourth season of *Desperate Housewives* is picked up at the beginning of the fifth season rather than reverted (forming an ellipsis rather than a flashforward) affects both narrative and characterization, as elaborated in chapter 2. Similarly, the second season of *Nurse Jackie* begins at what seems to be quite a while after the end

---

1. According to Alison Sharrock, "intratextuality is the phenomenon and the study of the relationship between elements within texts: it is concerned with structures such as ring composition, continuities, discontinuities, juxtapositions, story arcs and other repetitions of language, imagery, or idea, including gaps both in the hermeneutic circle and in the form of absent presences and roads not taken. It is interested in the problem of how texts are put together, by authors and readers, as unified wholes, or occasionally in creative disunities, and divided up into sections for ease of consumption or for other purposes" (2018, 15).

of the first season, perhaps several weeks or months, whereas the third season begins immediately after the moment at which the second season ends. A jump forward engenders a sense of catharsis, as if the tension mounting at the end of the previous season was resolved, whereas the immediate pickup after a season finale cliffhanger maintains narrative suspense. Respectively, the gap between seasons is set to launch the second season with a sense of a new beginning, designed to create distance from Jackie's previous season's transgression and incomprehension toward the season to come. In contrast, the tightness of the immediate pickup emphasizes Jackie's binding circumstances and consequent third season resistance.

The dual reading of the series as a whole and of the ties between episodes allows for an intricate structural analysis that explores the text as both unified and fragmentary. Though twenty-first-century serial structures are often correlated with the advancement and ubiquity of technology (Booth 2012) or with new modes of consumption (Johnson 2011), I focus on the serial form as such that is rooted in women's culture. Reading seriality vis-à-vis its historical textuality and not its contemporaneous contextually ties it to the genre of soap operas as, until roughly the 1980s, serial storytelling and narrative were exclusively practiced by soap operas. Most other television genres were episodic (Mittell 2015a). Relegated to daytime schedules and considered a women's genre, soap operas were deemed culturally inferior (Blumenthal 1997; Levine and Newman 2012) and, by extension, so was seriality (Levine and Newman 2012). During the 1980s, however, seriality found its way into a growing number of genres and was hybridized with episodic tales in a shift between seriality and episodicity that Mittell identifies as the inception of "narrative complexity" (2006). Thus, despite its contemporary omnipresence, television seriality at its purest is tied with inferiorized women's culture.

This gender politics of seriality is significant when investigating the generic conventions of the serial text, because, as critics have observed, the stretching of the serial structure affects the stretching of the narrative in a focus on relationships over action (Mittell 2007), a delay of narrative resolution (Modleski 1979), and a constant expansion of the story world (Allen 1985). If seriality is fundamentally a temporally resistant form—as it resists closure (Ndalianis 2005) and thereby complicates the narrative temporal flow—then its utilization in chick TV may offer feminist resistance to order. Bearing on this notion, I next demonstrate, using *The Real Housewives* docusoap franchise, that by reading chick TV via seriality, resistant antiheroinism emerges even if it is not explicitly presented in narration and characterization.

The Real Housewives: Serializing Antiheroinism, Antiheroinizing Seriality

The Real Housewives is a reality franchise, a docusoap that consists of ten separate installments, each following the lives of a cast of five to eight women who lead aspirational lifestyles in different American cities, with each having its own season count. The docusoap is a genre that, as reflected in its name, is rooted in the soap opera as applied to reality television. Specifically, *The Real Housewives* focuses on women, addressing their lives in terms of marriage and relationships, friendships and social life, work and sex. The series' emphasis on feminine performance, dialogue, and relationships renders it chick TV in a reality-TV incarnation. *The Real Housewives*' popularity, representation of wealth and privilege, and focus on women's issues have drawn criticism; it has been noted that the franchise is "problematic from a feminist political economic perspective" (Cox and Proffitt 2012, 299) as it promotes consumption, emphasizes appearance, and perpetuates gender roles (Squires 2014; Silverman 2015). Nevertheless, the franchise has also attracted academic interest and complex analyses of the show's realism (Lieber 2013) as well as its gender and class politics (Lee and Moscowitz 2013; Squires 2014). This chapter analyzes the effect that the expansion of the series into a franchise has had on its narrative and characterization and focuses on the correlation between the structure of the series and its representation of antiheroines.

The series' cast members are either socialites or aspiring socialites, mostly wealthy and often hedonistic and extroverted. Based on the characterization of the show's stars, this chapter searches for the ways in which the seriality of this ostensibly conservative show—celebrating capitalistic consumer culture and beauty myths—exposes and enhances instances of antiheroinism. These instances of antiheroinism arise across all antiheroinist continua but more specifically on the domestic continuum and the policing class continuum, in line with the women's social status. "Rich bitch" labeling, charges of vanity and narcissism associated with neglecting maternal duties (Lee and Moscowitz 2013), depictions of shallowness and superficiality, lack of restraint or loss of decorum are all villainized attributes that are antiheroinized when read through the franchise's form of seriality.[2]

The temporal structure under investigation here is the form of seriality by which *The Real Housewives* franchise is aired. Starting out as a monolithic series, *The Real Housewives* expanded into a franchise with several sister-installments based on the same premise but taking place in different locales. The franchise's expanding serial structure, as the following analyses illustrate, is an applicable affiliate to resistant antiheroinism as the structure of the series creates narrative disorder that has the potential to disrupt not only temporal but also patriarchal order.

Matrixial Seriality

The Real Housewives docusoap franchise was launched in 2006 with the first series, *The Real Housewives of Orange County*, setting out to depict the daily lives of mostly quadragenarian wives and mothers of mostly affluent, white backgrounds in Orange County, California. The success of this Orange County series led to the consequent production of several other shows based on the same premise: docusoaps following the lives of mostly middle-aged, affluent, and/or aspirational women

---

2. "Always gendered (female), always classed (leisure), and almost always racialized (white), she [the so-called rich bitch] functions at a cultural crossroads where class antagonisms can be articulated and traditional gender roles can be reasserted. The figure of the rich bitch fuels class-based contempt by reinforcing antifeminist tropes" (Lee and Moscowitz 2013, 65).

taking place in various other locations but aired on the same network (Bravo), thus sharing the same style, mode, and production techniques, such as editing and music. In 2008, *The Real Housewives of New York City* and *The Real Housewives of Atlanta* debuted, followed by *The Real Housewives of New Jersey* in 2009, *The Real Housewives of Beverly Hills* and *The Real Housewives of DC* in 2010, *The Real Housewives of Miami* in 2011, *The Real Housewives of Potomac* and *The Real Housewives of Dallas* in 2016, and *The Real Housewives of Salt Lake City* in 2020. Almost all these installments (excluding DC and Miami) are still running as of 2020. Thus, though starting as a monolithic series, *The Real Housewives of Orange County* expanded into a franchise with several "sister" installments that air parallel to each other rather than consecutively (Table 1). Thus, with the expansion of *The Real Housewives* into a multiform text, the airing formation of the series created a matrix-like system by which each installment continued to progress alongside its peers rather than any replacing another, thereby exhibiting a structure that expands "sideways" and not only forward.

A review of airing dates reveals that at first, new installments started airing after a sister installment's season concluded. The first season of the franchise's second installment, *The Real Housewives of New York City*, made its debut on the Bravo network in March 2008, after the third season of the Orange County original show had ended in January 2008.[3] The Atlanta installment aired in July 2008, after the New York City series concluded its first season in May of that year. As the years passed and the franchise expanded, however, installments began to overlap, with parallel episodes from different installments airing during the same week, some even on the same day.[4] For example, the

---

3. A preview special of the New York City installment was aired in January, some two months before the rest of the season started running.

4. My use of the "matrixial," though not derived directly from Bracha Ettinger's psychoanalytical theory of the "matrixial" (1995), echoes some features of Ettinger's theory. According to Ettinger, "the matrixial sphere is a space of encounters and their trails" (2001, 90), pertaining to psychoanalytic subjectivity. Matrixial seriality is similarly constructed of encounters—of texts—and their interplay with televisual

Table 1

Season progression of *The Real Housewives* installments

Year	RHoOC	RHoNYC	RHoA	RHoNJ	RHoDC	RHoBH	RHoM	RHoP	RHoD	RHoSLC
2006	1									
2007	2									
2008	3									
		1	1							
2009	4									
		2	2	1						
2010	5									
		3	3	2						
2011	6				1		1			
		4	4	3		2				
2012										
	7		5	4						
2013		5				3	2			
	8		6	5						
2014						4	3			
	9	6	7	6						
2015							5			
	10	7	8							
2016						6		1		
	11	8	9	7					1	
2017		9				7		2		
	12		10	8					2	
2018		10				8		3		
	13		11	9					3	
2019		11				9				
	14		12	10				4	4	
2020		12				10				
								5		1

← Horizontal Axis (parallel narratives across different installments aired over the same period of time) →

Vertical Axis (each installment's progression over years) ↓

RHoDC = Real Housewives of DC;   RHoBH = Real Housewives of Beverly Hills;
RHoA = Real Housewives of Atlanta;   RHoM = Real Housewives of Miami;
RHoOC = Real Housewives of Orange County;   RHoP = Real Housewives of Potomac;
RHoNYC = Real Housewives of New York City;   RHoD = Real Housewives of Dallas;
RHoNJ = Real Housewives of New Jersey;   RHoSLC = Real Housewives of Salt Lake City.

The numerals in the table signify the ordinal number of the season aired in the respective year in the headers column.

Note: Note that seasons last approximately three months, and the fact that certain seasons air on the same year does not necessarily mean they were featured along the same months or weeks. The seasons mentioned in the table are placed under the year in which the respective season premiered—as several of the seasons started airing at the end of a given year and ran through the beginning of the following year. More specific parallelizations will be explored in the following sections, pointing at installments that ran during the same months and weeks. The table is updated to 2020. As of the writing of this text, most installments are still running.

fourth *Real Housewives* installment, the one set in New Jersey, aired its first episode on the day of the antepenultimate episode of the third season of the New York installment, and the latter's three last episodes ran during the same three weeks of the former's first three, each on a different day of the week. The overlapping has itself expanded, so much so that May 2011 featured no fewer than three installments—Orange County's sixth season, New York's fourth, and New Jersey's third—running over the course of the same weeks, each debuting just a few weeks after the other and broadcast on a different day of the week. By 2012, the Atlanta and Beverly Hills series aired their fifth and third season premieres, respectively, just one week apart, with the rest of the two seasons essentially running parallel to each other, the first on Sundays and the second on Mondays (as was the case with Orange County's ninth season and New York City's sixth).

This mechanism resulted in a matrixial formation, by which, as of May 2010, there were nearly no *Real Housewives* episodes featured independently; almost every episode shared its airing week with a different, new episode (reruns are also interlaced in between new episodes during the week) from another installment of the series. The matrixial form, under which nearly every *Real Housewives* episode is textually linked to an episode from a different installment aired during the same week, renders the temporal layer of serialization particularly complex. By reading the lead women's characterization through the franchise's matrixial seriality, the meanings conveyed by the text are interpreted differently from the way in which interpretation of the separate episodes suggests. Moreover, as the following analyses demonstrate, matrixial interpretation of characterization is predominantly antiheroinizing.

In keeping with the expansion of the series, the narrative focus of the franchise's installments shifted from more individual storylines to more communal ones. In the first season of the first series—*The Real Housewives of Orange County*—most storylines were separate,

---

character subjectivity, that is, antiheroinism. Nevertheless, I diverge from Ettinger's theory in my use of the matrixial textual structure.

primarily following each woman with her family, in her home, at work, shopping, or running errands. A minority of scenes depicted instances of group activities, of all the women going shopping or attending parties. Later seasons, both of the Orange County installment and of the ones that followed it, have started focusing more on the relationships between the women of the cast and introducing a growing number of scenes in which at least two cast members were starring. In line with this shift, the 2015 seasons have not only been ruled by pair and group scenes, with fewer individual stories, but have also been ruled by storylines that involve relationships among the stars rather than their relationships with their respective family members or friends. The series' developing multiformity is also evidenced in production's growing use of long trips each cast takes (away from families and workplaces) and in the increased number of reunion episodes at the end of each season (with the cast gathering to discuss events from the season).

By multiplying its characters and series, *The Real Housewives* gradually grew to represent not only more stories of women but also more diverse ways with which to tackle women's issues. The multiplication, in both form and storytelling, thus suggests that despite the ostensible conservative perspective *The Real Housewives* may have on feminine performance—cast members all perform their femininity through conspicuous consumption, meticulous grooming regimens and fashion choices, heteronormative family values, etc.—it nevertheless brings forth various ways to deal with women's issues—from motherhood to body issues, from sexuality to divorce.

Thus, a matrix constructed of several serials, *The Real Housewives* franchise presents both separate storylines—with each character, episode, season, and installment—on the vertical axis, and serialized ones on the horizontal axis. Though each installment bears idiosyncrasies (local, ethnic, stylistic), the installments also share common threads that are interwoven through the branches in terms of themes and characterization.[5] The matrixial expansion can thus be used as an

5. The Atlanta installment features Black women, the Miami installment features Latinx women, and the New Jersey installment features Italian Americans. The

analytical tool to read narrative and characterization through their serial alignment rather than via isolated instances.

The Feminist Politics of the Matrix Form

It would be useful to locate the expansion of *The Real Housewives* within the context of contemporary perceptions of television complexity, specifically "complex TV," a term used by Mittell (2015a) to address US television series of the turn of the millennium. *The Real Housewives*, for that matter, belongs to a twenty-first-century phenomenon of expanding texts, as in the case of fictional multitexts, such as the *Law and Order* and the *CSI* franchises, the respective installments of which air in a parallel manner rather than consecutively, and the Marvel Comics Universe series, such as *Agents of S.H.I.E.L.D.* (2013–20), *The Defenders* (2017), *Daredevil* (2015–18), *Jessica Jones* (2015–19), *The Punisher* (2017–19), which share not only a narrative universe but also complete crossover episodes that present characters from more than one franchise series in the same episode (Johnson 2018).[6] Nevertheless, though contemporaneous propensity toward

---

casts of Beverly Hills, Orange County, New York City, and Dallas identify mainly as nonethnic whites, and the casts of DC, Potomac, and Salt Lake City offer more diverse casts. In late 2020, it was announced that *The Real Housewives of New York City* was to welcome its first Black cast member and *The Real Housewives of Beverly Hills* was to welcome the franchise's first Asian American cast member.

6. *The Real Housewives* launched a unique form in the reality television landscape, as most other reality franchises had consisted of national versions that are produced locally, as in the case of reality franchises such as *Big Brother*, *Survivor*, or *Must Love Kids*, or local versions that each only comprise one season, as in *The Real World* (1992–). The expansions of several other docusoaps into parallel reality franchises, such as *The Bachelor* (2002–) (spinoffs such as *The Bachelor Pad*, *Bachelor in Paradise*); *Million Dollar Listing* (*Los Angeles*, *New York*, *Miami*, *San Francisco*, 2006–); *Flip or Flop* (*Las Vegas*, *Atlanta*, *Nashville*, *Fort Worth*, *Chicago*, 2013–); and *Love & Hip Hop* (*New York*, *Atlanta*, *Hollywood*, *Miami*, 2011–) followed *The Real Housewives*. Furthermore, *Million Dollar Listing* and *Flip or Flop* rarely air episodes from different installments during the same week, as most seasons and episodes air during different months of the year.

complex seriality stands in the background of *The Real Housewives*' matrixial expansion, I focus on the multiformity of the franchise as such that is rooted in women's culture and its resistances (Lieber 2013), from women's serialized novels to television soap operas.

In referring to the seriality of soap operas, Tania Modleski notes they "do not end" (1979, 12), as they run daily and present continuous storylines, thereby delaying narrative closure. Modleski argues that soaps' delay of closure promotes "disorder" rather than (familial, social, patriarchal) order, thus indirectly resisting a perpetuation of hegemonic order. Soaps' disorder thereby signifies not only a challenge to narrative order but also to social order—a form of feminist resistance. If, according to Modleski, soaps suspend the return to order by presenting new questions in each episode instead of solving the ones raised in previous episodes, then *The Real Housewives* creates not only new episodes that pose new issues, but also new texts—more and more *Real Housewives* installments that exist in a parallel manner, each working to delay continuity, diverting the narrative flow of the vertical axis by deviating sideways horizontally. *The Real Housewives* not only inserts new questions into the singular, albeit meandering, narrative of each installment, it also interlaces new series "into" each of its series.

This formulation is most evident in the order by which episodes have aired since May 2010 with at least two separate seasons of different installments running parallel. By that configuration, *The Real Housewives* expands the soap-like delay of resolution by inserting additional, ostensibly unrelated narratives (as they belong to a different installment, featuring a different cast, locale, and arc) in the spaces between each season's episodes. In May 2011, for example, which introduced the first instance of three seasons running parallel, an episode of Orange County's late sixth season, airing on a Sunday, was followed by an episode of New Jersey's early third season on a Monday, and an episode of the middle of New York's fourth season on a Thursday, before the next Sunday introduced the next Orange County episode.

Unlike soap operas, which run continuously, *The Real Housewives* introduces endings to its narratives, as each installment is divided into seasons that often attempt to offer narrative closure, including follow-up reunion episodes that rehash seasonal conflicts in pursuit of resolution. Nevertheless, the franchise presents endless continuity as each season finale, as of 2008, is followed by an episode of a different installment of the franchise, which is either starting a new storyline or picking one up in medias res. This resistance to closure, which signifies a feminist resistance to a return to order, can first be observed in the shift of the series from a monolithic text into a multitext, with the airing of the New York City preview special, which marked the end of *The Real Housewives of Orange County* as a singular text and turned it into part of a franchise. On January 22, 2008, Orange County's third season finale was followed by the New York City preview special, which was scheduled immediately after the Orange County finale concluded on the same channel.

The shift of the series from a monolithic text into a multitext started with the airing of the New York City preview special, which marked the end of *The Real Housewives of Orange County* as a singular text and turned it into a part of a franchise. On January 22, 2008, the Orange County's third season finale was aired at 8:00 p.m. and was followed by New York City's preview special at 9:00 p.m.[7] The Orange County finale focused on two main events as the first half of the episode was dedicated to the wedding of cast member Lauri Waring, about to become Lauri Peterson, and the second half was dedicated to a party hosted a week later by another cast member, Jeana Keough. The season thus did not end with the union of one woman with one man—as happy-ending resolutions often do—but with the collectivity of a group of women. The episode ends with all

---

7. Of course, the airing of the New York preview special immediately following the Orange County finale stems from production's economic desire to lure in Orange County viewers to watch the New York show, but once the two were thusly joined they essentially turned into two incarnations of a common media entity.

the women, two of whom are single, standing in a circle and chatting, cocktails in their hands. "We all are kind of a little family," the voice of cast member Tammy Knickerbocker is heard against the backdrop of the women hugging each other at the party. "We're not perfect; we all have our issues. We really are just women who really care about our children and try to be there for each other." The last shot freezes the six together. This sequence, the final one before the text becomes a multitext, sets the tone of the franchise to come, focusing on the ties between the women rather than on each of the women separately (or between each woman and her partner). Though often the ties between the women result in clashes, the collectivity and multiplicity remain in the foreground.

The choice to end the Orange County third season finale in a women's gathering in which all the women are dressed casually rather than in a wedding in which one of the women is the focus of the event is in itself telling of the gradually more multifarious character the series demonstrates. More than that, the choice to follow the Orange County finale with the New York installment's preview further emphasizes the series' multiplicity-oriented structure, as Lauri Waring Peterson's fairytale-like wedding in the Orange County finale is not only followed by a nonhierarchical scenario, but also by the tales of a new group of women—the "real housewives" of New York City.[8]

After the Orange County finale approaches chrononormative romantic resolution but then unsettles it, the narratives of New York City add further breaks and detours to the myth of happily ever after. Read together, the two episodes—the Orange County Finale and the New York City preview—comprise a new text, the formation of which complicates the separate narrative of each episode. To use Modleski's words, if Lauri's wedding could be said to signify the "end of expectation" and a "return to order" (1979, 29), then the ending scene of

---

8. Lauri resonates the marriage-as-happy-ending convention, noting, "I'm so looking forward to being Mrs. George Peterson . . . our romance and wedding is like a fairytale come to life."

the Orange County episode represents a disruption to that order, with its tales of breakup (cast member Quinn's), parenting issues (Lauri's and Jeana's), and men-less women's comradery (the closing shot of the episode is of the women standing next to each other). Moreover, the happily-ever-after ending is not only usurped by a different ending but is also stripped of its signification as an ending in that it is immediately followed by a new beginning—that of the New York preview. The introduction of a new episode, a new cast, a new city, and new practices (including one self-proclaimed "runaway bride") multiplies the franchise's escape from order and resistance to narrative resolution by restarting narrative conflict and disorder.

Interestingly, when *The Real Housewives* was no longer a monolithic progressive narrative but a matrixially expanding narrative, it seemed to be less tolerant to happy-ending wedding narratives, as if it were unable to contain endings. Following the Orange County third season finale's featuring of Lauri's fairytale wedding, almost all of *The Real Housewives* tales of matrimony were "outsourced" from the main text. Atlanta's Kandi Burruss (*Kandi's Wedding*, 2014), Kim Zolciak Biermann (*Don't Be Tardy*, 2012–20), and NeNe Leaks (*I Dream of NeNe: The Wedding*, 2013) all featured their weddings in spin-off shows rather than on the main series, as did New York's Bethenny Frankel (*Bethenny Ever After*, 2010–12), and Orange County's Tamra Barney Judge (*Tamra's OC Wedding*, 2013). Seeing as weddings epitomize the happy-ending convention, the "outsourcing" of the romantic resolution of weddings emphasizes the franchise's matrixial seriality's delay of closure and resistance to order.[9]

Ties across the franchise's matrixial seriality thus work to promote feminist resistance to narrative and patriarchal order by reigniting disorder once resolution is underway. The following sections conduct a matrixial reading that focuses on characterization in consecutive

---

9. Certainly, the production decision to "outsource" wedding narratives from the main series into designated spin-off series has economic interests at its base, but it is nonetheless congruent with the text's narrative aspirations.

episodes of separate installments, suggesting that reading characterization through matrixial seriality engenders antiheroinization tied to the matrixial structure's feminist resistance.[10]

The Real Housewives' Matrixial Antiheroinism

Reading *The Real Housewives* matrixially works to complicate the reading of each installment and of each episode independently. Of course, the message of many *Real Housewives* scenes is sometimes reversed within a single installment or even within a single episode, echoed, for example, in the mechanism of intentionally coded irony utilized by the Bravo network in its various productions, using editing and tone to contrast content (the cited "Bravo wink," Lee and Moscowitz 2013, 67). However, contrasts on the vertical axis, that is along the flow of a single installment, are irony-driven disorientations that are used as a conscious and intentional technique, promoted by production and work to vilify the stars of the franchise (Lee and Moscowitz 2013). Conversely, contrasts on the horizontal axis, namely, such that run through parallel episodes of different installments, are driven by the text itself, by the configuration of the airing of episodes

---

10. Per the focus of this book, I conduct a textual analysis of *The Real Housewives*' airing formation rather than a contextual or institutional analysis. It is nevertheless relevant to address the fact that episodes tied via the franchise's matrixial seriality are not only interlinked textually but also contextually, as production and reception practices reveal that all installments are perceived as part of the same narrative "universe" (much like the *Arrowverse* or the *CSI*-universe). As part of the ever-expanding *Real Housewives* matrix, the informed popular culture aficionado is encouraged to follow all installments to keep up with topical cultural knowledge, fueled by talk shows, celebrity magazines, and entertainment websites (Jennings 2019) that merge the franchise's diegetic narratives with extratextual gossip. Consequently, many fans are known to watch episodes of numerous installments across the franchise (Cassilo 2018), and though not all watch episodes as they air, many catch up on the same week (Liberman 2015), thus following the trajectory of the matrixial airing configuration despite changes in the television viewing experience (with audiences consuming television neither at the time nor necessarily in the sequence of broadcasting).

and not by production interests, and therefore have the potential to work against the narrative vilification of the cast members rather than to promote it.

Resistance on the Domestic Continuum

Much of the characterization of the franchise centers on the maintenance of the domestic continuum and the policing of the class continuum. Though resistance on both these continua appears along the vertical axis (either with overdoing domesticity or resisting it, either with unruliness or snobbery), matrixial reading antiheroinizes the often villainized women of *The Real Housewives*. A distinct example of the horizontal axis's antiheroinization of the vertical axis's flow on the domestic continuum can be seen in the parallel 2012 seasons of Atlanta and Beverly Hills. The November 19 episode of the Beverly Hills installment (season 3, episode 3) presents David, the husband of cast member Yolanda Foster, as he discusses his wife in a confessional. "Yolanda as a hostess is nothing short of stunning and spectacular," he notes, adding, "I'm shocked now at how many women don't know how to be a great homemaker and hostess. She just gets everything right without being froufrou, because I hate hate hate froufrou." Read for its own sake, David's comment encapsulates a bind of feminine performance—in order to be a great homemaker and hostess, key features of feminine performance, a woman must do it "just right." Not being a "great homemaker and hostess" is criticized, and overdoing it, that is, doing it to the point of "froufrou" is also, as David's comment illustrates, criticized. David's remark signifies the plight of feminine performance: a woman would be chastised for underdoing her feminine performance—in this on the domestic continuum—as well as for overdoing it, and the "right" amount will always remain arbitrary and elusive (Butler 1988).[11]

 11. This echoes the words of Judith Butler, who notes that "performing one's gender wrong initiates a set of punishments both obvious and indirect, and performing it well provides the reassurance that there is an essentialism of gender identity

Read vertically, the Beverly Hills scene presents a traditional gender role commentary, ostensibly perpetuating patriarchal rule. However, when read horizontally, against the series' parallel representations of the domestic obligations of feminine performance, David's comment, crosscut with footage of the lavish dinner party his wife has organized, serving staff included, gains additional, antiheroinist layers. On November 25, a day before the next Beverly Hills episode was aired, the fourth episode of Atlanta's fifth season was broadcast and featured cast member Kenya Moore ordering food, removing it from its containers, and rushing to plate it before her boyfriend arrives. When he enters her house, she pretends to have made the food herself. "It took me forever to make this meal," she tells him, "but I'm just trying to focus more on, you know, family life, and trying to get myself more accustomed to being wifey, being at home, being a mother." The Atlanta scene plays against the Beverly Hills scene, intertextualizing with David's comment—according to which women must perform femininity (in this case as homemaker and hostess) "just right"—and in a sense satirizing it by exposing that being "wifey" demands time and resources as well as accuracy in avoiding both underdoing and overdoing it.

The Atlanta scene exposes the mechanism behind the "great homemaker and hostess" who cannot always do it "right" and emphasizes the arbitrariness and constructedness of successful feminine performance. Many of the women in the show are represented as not doing "it" "right," as they often underdo their feminine performances (in terms of characterization and actions) or overdo it (froufrouing it, so to speak). In this case, the matrixial form creates comparative representations of different positionalities along the domestic continuum. When read alongside each other, David's articulation of the clasp of feminine performance is revisited via Kenya's mis-performance of it.

---

after all. That this reassurance is so easily displaced by anxiety, that culture so readily punishes or marginalizes those who fail to perform the illusion of gender essentialism should be sign enough that on some level there is social knowledge that the truth or falsity of gender is only socially compelled and in no sense ontologically necessitated" (1988, 528).

In that way, parallel episodes and seasons work to negate, criticize, scrutinize, and complement coextensive representations.

Read independently, the Kenya sequence is framed as comic, but read alongside Yolanda's sequence, it becomes a tale of unintentional feminist criticism regarding the binds of femininity. In a different manner from the work of vilifying irony that is intentionally coded into the franchise's episodes, marked by playful music in Kenya's sequence and by mockery-inducing editing in Yolanda's sequence (showing she does not do everything "just right" by herself but, rather, has a full staff to assist her), the text's matrixial complication of the discourse of housewifery and feminine performance offers antiheroinist criticism of patriarchal order itself rather than of the women who struggle to maintain it. Via matrixial analysis, Yolanda's vertical-axis heroinization is problematized, and Kenya's vertical-axis vilification is reframed into antiheroinism as her mocked simulation of domestic propriety on the vertical axis becomes a deconstruction of feminine performance in the comparative horizontal axis, thus exposing the arbitrary demands of patriarchal order and effectively resisting their naturalized control. Thus, while the vertical axis of the franchise tends to favor "normative conceptions of class and gender" (Lee and Moscowitz 2013, 65), under which the "real housewives" are "figures of scorn and pity" (Lee and Moscowitz 2013, 78), the horizontal axis works to antiheroinize, challenge, and complicate said "normative conceptions of class and gender."

Significantly, though the horizontal axis complicates the reading of the vertical axis's irony with a more complex perception of feminine performance as arbitrary and constructed, the Kenya/Yolanda comparison may also perpetuate a racial hierarchy by which white affluent women's performance of femininity manages to maintain hegemonic order, exemplified in Yolanda's performance, whereas the performance of less privileged women of color does not gain access to order, as is represented in Kenya's performance. Such a reading renders the matrix's potential disorder as racially regressive despite its feminist aspirations. Indeed, the franchise at times perpetuates social stereotypes, including those regarding race and gender, and effects conservative ideologies on the vertical axis. Still, the matrixial ties between the episodes open the possibility to create a complex feminist resistance to order.[12]

For that matter, the franchise is rife with examples of white women undoing feminine performance on the domestic continuum, from New York's LuAnn de Lesseps's various "failures" at nurturing motherhood, as she is scorned for prioritizing her self-indulgence over her familial obligations, to Beverly Hills's Lisa Rinna's declarations regarding her lacking domestic skills. Relatedly, the tenth season premiere of Atlanta (2017) features Kenya's "fairytale ending," as she has just gotten married, followed by an Orange County episode, the next day, revealing the disintegration of Shannon Beador's marriage, insinuating her "failed" feminine performance as wife and lover. Read vertically, Kenya's fairytale ending can work as a "return to order," inverting her previous "failed" feminine performances. Read horizontally, however, Kenya's happy ending is compared with its successive matrixial unit, the Orange County episode of white marital and familial disorder.[13] In this case, it is the woman of color who is the text's signifier of order.

Similarly, the two reunion episodes of Orange County's twelfth season (2017) include many instances of criticism of many cast

---

12. For more on the racial complexities of *The Real Housewives*' "unladylike" conduct, see Kristen Warner (2015), who shows how the racialized "ratchet" behavior of Black women in reality TV, including *The Real Housewives of Atlanta*, serves as a way to make visible the often invisible body of Black women and invites viewers' identification with excessive self-expression. Ratchet behavior in these images, Warner articulates, forms an affective outlet for the Black woman viewer who would avoid such behavior in her day-to-day so as to maintain respectability.

13. Further than that, the same week's episode of the New Jersey installment addressed the "alternative" relationship of Dolores, who is living with her ex-husbands, demonstrating the various versions of heterosexual reunions, including those that overturn the marriage-as-happy-ending convention. When read together, the three early November 2017 *Real Housewives* examples work to reveal the constructedness of the social rite of marriage and challenge its traditional perpetuation of patriarchal order.

members' forms of motherhood, including self-criticism, as Shannon Beador blames herself for neglecting her maternal duties during marital hardship; familial criticism, as Tamra Judge's daughter, the reunion host notes, accuses her mother "of putting yourself and your fame and your bank account and your reputation before" her family's wellbeing; and social criticism, as castmates slam Meghan King Edmonds, insinuating she should focus more on taking care of her baby than on other pursuits. The fourth episode of Atlanta's tenth season is sandwiched between these two reunion episodes and features Kandi Burruss expressing her dedication to motherhood as she laments having to leave her children to go to work, noting, "I love being successful, but what I want the most is to be a great mom to my kids." A vertical reading of the Atlanta episode raises Kandi's commitment to her family and prioritization of motherhood over career as an aspiration toward order (both narrative and patriarchal). However, when reading the episodes horizontally, in considering the franchise units in the order by which they were aired—first the Orange County reunion episode portraying women who "fail" in terms of the feminine demand for self-sacrifice for the sake of family and motherhood, then the Atlanta episode addressing the prioritizing of the feminine role of motherhood over other pursuits, and then the second Orange County reunion episode continually portraying women who "fail" their feminine performance—the Orange County and Atlanta episodes' performances and mis-performances are intertwined to create narrative disorder. The horizontal reading thus emphasizes the elusiveness of doing motherhood "just right," as some of the Orange County women share heartfelt stories, which reposition Kandi's commitment as hard to maintain, at least in a consistent manner.

In this case, the tales of the white Californian women signify disorder whereas the tale of the Southern Black woman is that which stands for order. However, it is the comparison between the two that creates a more complex perception of the arbitrariness and constructedness of hegemonic order. Thus, the vertical axis of *The Real Housewives* may judge "women transgressing their roles as mothers and caregivers" (Lee and Moscowitz 2013, 80) in tone, music, and editing, whether through comic irony, as in the case of Kenya's cooking; implied mockery, as in the case of LuAnn's socializing; explicit criticism, as in the case of the criticism toward the motherhood of the Orange County women; or unequivocal demonization, as in some portrayal of Beverly Hills's Carlton Gebbia.[14] The horizontal axis of the franchise, however, generates complex textual comparisons regarding the trials of femininity, working to challenge the vertical axis's occasional oppressive gender politics and resisting not only narrative closure but also traditional social order. The horizontal axis thus works to antiheroinize the women of *The Real Housewives* as it repositions their singular "failures" to fulfill social expectations of feminine performance as a matrixial web of resistances to the social order.

Resistance on the Class Continuum

In a similar manner to the way in which the domestic continuum is maintained on the vertical axis and antiheroinized on the horizontal axis, the maintenance of decorum on the class continuum is constantly interrupted in each installment's narrative but is further problematized, in fact antiheroinized, by the matrixial structure's feminist resistance. Much of the criticism against the franchise stems from the women's frequent fighting (Spinelli 2014; Jacobs 2018), which is perceived to be perpetuating negative stereotypes of women as catty, petty, boorish, or hysterical (Lee and Moscowitz 2013). The soap-like stretch of the narrative of *The Real Housewives*, however, often dives into the circumstances behind these fights, implying that women's conflict and anger are a justified response to oppressive

---

14. Though Lee and Moscowitz address only the New York installment, many of their analyses are relevant to the franchise as a whole, most certainly in terms of the text's often conscious scapegoating and mockery of cast members, specifically pertaining to the domestic continuum, with women "who transgress the traditional gender roles of supportive friend, nurturing mother, doting wife, and ceaseless caretaker" (2013, 65).

circumstances.[15] Furthermore, the franchise's complex matrixial form works to intensify the antiheroinist renegotiation of feminine performance on the class continuum that sometimes emerges on the vertical axis.

Though "femininity" and the performativity that validates it are elusive and changing according to time, place, age, race, and social standing, the stars of *The Real Housewives* often refer to the concept of "the lady" as the emblem of aspired feminine conduct. Alexandra Allan correlates the discourse of eighteenth-century etiquette guides to the emergence of ideals of feminine performance, "such as calmness, ease, restraint and luxurious decoration" (2009, 146). These attributes still stand as signifiers of proper feminine performance in *The Real Housewives*, and the women of the franchise both revere them and continuously negotiate them. In *The Real Housewives of Atlanta*'s season three premiere, for example, cast member Phaedra Parks responds to castmate NeNe Leaks's lashing out at a mutual friend by saying "NeNe was really out of control. As a lady, that was just shameful," and in the New York installment's first season's fourth episode, cast member Ramona Singer describes castmate Jill Zarin leaving an event due to less-than-desirable seating arrangements as "not a normal reaction, or ladylike, or classy, or elegant." These are only two of many examples that work to define the ways in which the women judge themselves and others as their class aspirations define their form of feminine performance.

The class continuum is thus a constant regulator as the women in the series are characterized by their upper-class affiliation and must preserve their status as such to remain within the narrative premise of the show. Reading "failures" to maintain decorum, so often criticized both in the text and extratextually, across parallel representations along the horizontal axis antiheroinizes the vilified instances because

---

15. Julie Wilhelm suggests, for example, that "the franchise portrays women's social aggression to be the consequence of economic insecurity" (2013, 41).

it exposes how systematic the regulation of feminine performance is. Fissures in the performance of feminine decorum appear in the fourteenth episode of the Atlanta installment's third season as the fiancé of cast member Cynthia Bailey announces he has officially shut down his restaurant—the couple's only source of income. Disappointed that her partner in life and business had thus far kept the restaurant's decline a secret from her and upset that she may not make payments for her fast-approaching wedding, Cynthia expresses anger and distress at her partner. When her fiancé, frustrated with her response, suggests that she not worry, she exclaims: "Don't make me feel like I don't have the right to be genuinely devastated that, like, everything is going to hell right now." Having no control over the household finances and attaining no knowledge of her economic state, Cynthia refuses to suffer silently and justifies her expressive frustration.

In and of itself, this scene brings to the foreground feminist issues of a woman's right to express herself and be able to secure her finances. However, the notion of the necessity to break feminine performance, opt for antiheroinism, and throw restraint to the wind in order to protect oneself is magnified via the series' matrixial structure. The Atlanta installment's third season, as part of which the episode mentioned above was aired, ran parallel to the first season of the Beverly Hills installment, the former on Mondays and later on Sundays, the latter on Thursdays and later on Tuesdays, both from October 2010 to February 2011. During the Beverly Hills season, the issue of unladylike anger also appears, as a heated argument between two castmates—Camille Grammer and Kyle Richards—embodies the social perception of women's break of decorum and expression of anger.

In two consecutive episodes, Kyle signifies the "unladylike" angry woman, who, according to Camille, and the majority of the society that surrounds her, "lost her cool" when she expressed her anger. Camille, on the other hand, is portrayed as the epitome of ladylike restraint, noting at a confessional, regarding Kyle's outburst, "I knew I was winning. I just know, come on. You know, the person that remains in control is the one that wins. She lost her cool. Sorry, Kyle, you lose" (Beverly Hills, season 1, episode 5). The argument between the two castmates quickly shifts from being about who-said-what and becomes, at least for Camille, about keeping her cool. Camille's comments echo the social demands of women to restrain their emotions, especially those who desire upper-class acceptance and are urged to exhibit the characteristics of a lady.

The parallel presentation of Atlanta's Cynthia's expression of anger with Beverly Hills's Kyle's expression of anger and Camille's lack of expression essentially makes each installment commentary for the other. If unladylike anger is, according to social and status obligations, a form of deviation from proper feminine performance, then the representation of multiple, parallel instances of women's improper response to oppression or conflict threatens both narrative and patriarchal order. These instances of antiheroinism—of negotiating the expectation for restraint with the desire to express one's frustration—break the linear progression of each installment and divert narrative attention. Instead of aspiring toward a resolution of the narrative disorder—in the form of reconciliation between Cynthia and her fiancé and between Kyle and Camille or in the form of restraining the straying antiheroines—the text redirects the narrative to parallel tales of divergence from patriarchal order, thus maintaining the resistance to order.

When read together, Beverly Hills's first season and Atlanta's third season present a matrixial complex comment about the silencing of women, proposing that a woman's unladylike behavior can serve as an antiheroic reclaiming of power and agency. The parallel presentation of the two story arcs in the parallel seasons creates a more complex statement on women's oppression and expression, as Cynthia's antiheroinist refusal to calmly accept her oppression and to resist it by breaking ladylike decorum is further antiheroinized by Camille's comments. Not only that, but Cynthia's expression of anger reflects Camille's struggle with expression as Camille's own marriage disintegrates throughout the season while she remains silent on the subject. Through matrixiality, Cynthia's expression of anger and vindication of her right to express it are inscribed in the text in a way that gradually impacts Camille's perception. By the end of the season, Camille would break her propriety in addressing her marital frustrations. Camille is thus antiheroinized via the franchise's matrixial seriality, promoting feminist resistance to the requirement to maintain decorum despite circumstances.

The women of *The Real Housewives* are not only antiheroines because they fail at or overdo domesticity (bad hostess/froufrou), or because they fail or overdo upper-class decorum (unladylike/snob). They are also antiheroines because in their negotiation of the demands of feminine performance—and more so in the comparative analysis of parallel instances of their negotiation of feminine performance—they often reveal social contradictions in general and such that bind women in particular. When read matrixially, across parallel episodes on the horizontal axis and not only along the episodic narrative flow of the vertical axis, the "housewives'" transgressions stop being single instances of misconduct and become part of a matrix of antiheroinisms more indicative of the arbitrary and oppressive demands of the society that surrounds the women than of their singular "failures" to adhere to social demands.

When read matrixially, the experiences of the "housewives" can no longer be perceived as isolated instances of women's lives. Instead, they become a multilayered account of feminine performances and antiheroinist feminist resistances. Even when progression toward resolution and order is underway on the vertical axis, with "proper" feminine performance, weddings, or domestic bliss, the horizontal axis's disruption and digressions cause the narrative to suspend progression, delay closure, and resist order. Behind the ostensibly trivial aspects of the franchise's vertical axis's high-class women's stories, from shopping to parties, *The Real Housewives*' matrixiality reveals and deconstructs social paradigms and gender biases. *The Real Housewives*' unique matrix textuality, in a sense a form of serialized seriality, may serve as an epitomic study of seriality, a concentrated example through which to examine the power of textuality to challenge and reshape the viewpoints that are communicated through story alone. *The Real Housewives*' matrixial textual disorder bears feminist potential in its antiheroinist resistance to order and may work to overturn the sometimes "problematic" gender politics each installment may reflect independently.

Serial Antiheroinism

Though *The Real Housewives*' matrixial structure promotes a double reading that uncovers the text's antiheroinism, monolithic chick TV seriality (rather than franchise/matrix) also bears the potential for a resistant and antiheroinizing reading. The ties between a season finale and the next season premiere, for example, as mentioned at the beginning of this chapter, affect the series tone and characterization. In this way, season finales become significant links in the serial form as scenes that end a season initially function as a final note but are repurposed if followed by a new season, becoming intermediary.

Particularly interesting in that regard are clichéd endings that close a season, such as the happy-ending convention that perpetually accompanies plots in western culture by ending stories in marriage or a romantic union and thus reaffirming the social order (Boone 1987; MacDowell 2013). According to convention, the romantic union is the pinnacle of the narrative, the peak point to which the story aspires. Consequently, if a wedding concludes a film, it functions as the event from which "nothing of interest—no meaningful change, in other words—was expected to happen" (Elliott 2008, 46). However, if a wedding concludes a series' season that is followed by another season, it becomes a plot feature rather than a plot conclusion.

Being a part of chick culture's thematic content, the romantic pursuit often finds its way into chick TV, with weddings a critical part of the story rather than its culmination. Thus weddings are recast from the event to which the narrative aspires into one of many other life events. Just as *The Real Housewives of Orange County*'s first season's ending wedding serves as only a temporary perpetuation of hegemonic order before the duration of the text refuels disorder, so do other serialized chick TV season finales. *Grey's Anatomy*, for instance, often features weddings that produce a sense of resolution but are intermingled with dramatic disorder—romantic or otherwise. Pertinently, the first season finale of *Girls* ("She Did," season 1, episode 10) features a wedding at the end of the episode between Jessa, one of the main characters, and Thomas. However, the second season sees the married couple break up. Though the first season frames the wedding as a final note, a perpetuation of order and validation of chrononormativity, the regeneration of the narrative in the second season in fact works to dismantle the validation of chrononormativity with a return to disorder. The story keeps going; the wedding does not set the final tone.

Similarly, the second season finale of *Girls* ("Together," season 2, episode 10) presents a romantic chase—the staple of so many Hollywood romantic comedies and a generic reference point in the chick TV framework—in which one of the romantic protagonists runs to catch the other before he or she gets married to someone else or leave the country or surrender to any other dramatic, seemingly irreversible obstacle. In the finale, Adam, the estranged romantic interest of protagonist Hannah, realizes Hannah is both sick and misses him and runs through the streets of Brooklyn to reunite with her. The sequence is all pathos and emotion, including sentimental romantic music in a generally cynical—or at least too self-aware to be melodramatic—series, as Adam and Hannah converse over video-chat while he is running toward her, chest bare, in New York streets. He eventually arrives at her apartment, kicks the door down, and picks her up from her bed to hold her.

Though this episode utilizes the traditional, order-perpetuating, chrononormative happy-ending convention of a couple's reunion, the fact that it is placed in the middle of the series rather than in its ending reconfigures the structure of the series as a whole from a text that restores order to such that approaches it but then continuously destabilizes it. Though the second season finale positions Hannah as a romantic heroine, the temporality of seriality, which restarts disorder at the beginning of the following season, engenders resistance to chrononormative narrative order, thus rendering Hannah a romantic antiheroine.

This convention is, of course, not new. Significantly, the generic ancestor of chick TV—the soap opera—has perpetually introduced weddings as ostensible resolution toward order that soon gives way to disorder. Nevertheless, the complex narrative of twenty-first-century television, with its shift between episodicity and seriality (Mittell 2015a), introduces endings, which the soap opera does not (Modleski 1979). In the soap opera, all narrative movement toward resolution is unsettled as the text is stretched out for years, but in the series, the function of an ending is only realized with the beginning of the next unit—episode/season. The second season finale of *Girls* was produced after the third season was okayed (Panos 2012), meaning that the text knowingly places a conventional ending as a plot twist rather than a plot ending, turning it from validation of order to manipulation of order. There are other cases, however, in which the ending-as-middle construct is the extratextual result of the television production economy, as often creators opt to conclude a season with an ending scene (rather than leaving loose ends or concluding with a cliffhanger) in case the series will not be picked up for another season (Mittell 2015a). In case the series is renewed, the ending is rerouted and becomes a midpoint. This state of affairs creates a proliferation of season finales that attempt at tying up loose ends that are then unraveled again in the next season.

To be sure, seriality at its basic structure resists closure (Creeber 2004; Ndalianis 2005; Mittell 2015a), and the ending that is reframed as a midpoint appears in many television texts and not only chick TV, sometimes with artistic intent and sometimes by force of circumstances. Still, the happy ending is embedded in the chick TV text by its affiliation with the oft-romantic chick culture, and its problematization of the convention is part of its antiheroinizing resistance to narrative and patriarchal order. That chick TV tends to represent the happy ending in a resistant manner—hinted at but continually deferred by the force of the serial structure—is a form of antiheroinist feminist resistance that is generated by the temporality of television seriality.

Other resistances that the serial structure offers stem from serial ties around an antiheroinizing theme, form, or narrative device that connects episodes outside their scheduled order, as can be seen in the ties analyzed in previous chapters, such as those between *Girls'* death episodes, *Nurse Jackie*'s reverie episodes, or *Grey's Anatomy*'s flashback episodes. The antiheroinizing threads between (not necessarily consecutive) episodes breed an interpretation of the text that is different from the interpretation that arises from the linear narrative flow. Seriality thus lends itself to temporal play, offering in the creases of the text—the intratextual relationship between the singular unit (episode) and the whole (series)—potential for feminist resistance.

The structure of seriality as potential for temporal and antiheroinist resistance brings about temporal delay that is different from implicit resistance to order in the intradiegetic level (story-within-story, reverie, confessional) or from explicit deviation from order in the diegesis (flashes). Principally, the temporal resistance of seriality is inherent in its stretching structure that delays closure. More so than that—because it is a wider temporal layer than intradiegetic or diegetic temporalities—the intratextual temporality of seriality is shaped by the temporal resistance of the more atomic textual layers. If the diegesis exhibits explicit antiheroinist resistance to or deviation from order, an intratextual reading may enhance it via comparative analyses with other parts of the diegesis, be they explicitly resistant or not. Conversely, if the diegesis perpetuates hegemonic order, a comparative intratextual analysis may expose the arbitrariness and constructedness of the hegemonic order.

The temporal layer of seriality thus serializes delays, resistances, and deviations, and focuses on the ties between episodes as offering an additional interpretive level of the text beyond the diegesis. The next and final chapter addresses the most expansive layer of television temporality, that of intertextuality. Following analyses of the intraepisodic, the episodic, and the serial, the upcoming discussion looks into intertextual repetitions between antiheroines in twenty-first-century chick TV and argues that, via intertextuality, antiheroinism is bolstered, thus essentially formulating an alternative narrative and social order.

4
Rewriting

Previous chapters explored several forms of feminist resistance via the correlation between temporal complexity and antiheroinism. Chapter 1 addressed the implicit resistance of intradiegetic devices and explored the interplay of temporal complexity and antiheroinism in the televisual language—the delay of reverie, story-within-story, fantasy, simulation of liveness, and the docusoap confessional—and the way in which this interplay works to resist chrononormativity and patriarchal order. Chapter 2 investigated the deviation from narrative order of flashes (flashback, flashforward, and flash-sideways) as a form of explicit temporal-antiheroinist resistance that not only delays hegemonic order but also deviates from it. Chapter 3 focused on the serialization of textual delays and deviations, both implicit and explicit, reading resistances in the correlation between antiheroinism and the temporality of seriality (intratextuality, matrixialization) and arguing that the comparative value of various, often contradicting, performances of femininity generates antiheroinism and, thus, resistance to order. This chapter expands the investigation of antiheroines and temporality by exploring forms of antiheroinism and resistance that stem from intertextual repetition. I focus on the cumulative value of intertextualizing antiheroines such that it essentially works to rewrite televisual order in presenting an alternative televisual realm in which antiheroinist order is in reign.[1]

---

1. The analyses in this chapter utilize a more rhizomatic approach than the intratextual or matrixial analysis of seriality, as the chapter studies intertextual ties of "all directions" (Deleuze and Guattari 2003, 7) rather than in accordance with the movement of the serial form.

The Temporality of Intertextuality: Repetition and Resistance

Elizabeth Alsop argues that portrayals of women in the post-network era are often organized by a "rhetoric of sisterhood" (2019, 1026), with television series governed by "sororities," such as *Orange Is the New Black* (2013–19) and *Big Little Lies* (2017–19).[2] The focus of the series on women collectives, Alsop asserts, serves as "counterprogramming" to the era's purported predominance of men antiheroes. In this chapter, I read the "sisterhood" showcased in twenty-first-century US televisual representations as appearing not only in series but also across them. Not only do groups of women in specific series form a sisterhood against patriarchal culture, so do all resistant women, that is, antiheroines, form a sisterhood across various series, intertextually. Consequently, intertextual ties between antiheroines of different series have the potential to bolster the resistance exerted by each antiheroine individually.

Intertextuality, coined by Kristeva, refers to the perception that "every signifying practice is a field of transpositions of various signifying systems," and that a text's "'place' of enunciation and its denoted 'object' are never single, complete and identical to themselves, but always plural, shattered, capable of being tabulated" (1984, 60). Perceiving text thus—as permeable and constantly open to reorganization through exchanges with other texts—bears the potential for a radical rereading, a reading of a text against itself and the social systems under which it was produced. More specifically, Kristeva notes, intertextuality creates "transformation" through both "opposition and analogy" (1980, 89), which reflects textual feminist resistance, striving to transform patriarchal narratives through opposing their traditional binds (via antiheroinism and nonchrononormativity, for

---

2. Popularized by Amanda Lotz (2007), the "post-network era" relates to early twenty-first-century US television, which is characterized, according to Lotz, by increased viewer access to television content provided by more platforms that offer consumer control.

example) and creating ties of semblance between the resisting entities (intertextualizing antiheroines and resistant temporal constructs).

Intertextuality's capacity for resistance is congruent with its temporal properties, as it is a form of repetition (Eco 1985) correlated with circularity and return (and consequently with "women's time," Kristeva 1981; Modleski 2002) and thus challenges chrononormativity. Intertextuality as a temporal form that resists narrative linearity and progression reflects scholarly discourse on the powers of textual repetition as "transgression" (Deleuze 1994, 3). Correspondingly, intertextual repetition between defiant women undermines hegemonic authority (Zanger 2006, 113). Anat Zanger states that the repetition of characteristics of women "who transgress social roles" (2006, 53) works to "represent the forbidden spaces where . . . woman refuses to conform to the symbolic order. While using the dialectic of repetitions and differences as their motivating force," she stresses, "these persistently performative rewritings are marked 'holes' in the symbolic order" (128). Via repetition, the seams that make up women characters' repetitive tropes and stereotypes become visible. Repetition contributes, according to Judith Butler, to a recontextualization of that which has been determined by essentializing hegemonic culture, bearing the capacity to displace seemingly determinate gender identities.[3] "The function of repetition is to render the structure of the myth apparent," Lévi-Strauss asserts (1976, 229), addressing a repetition that does not perpetuate but, rather, transforms.

The intertextual repetition of chick TV antiheroines has the power to transform narrative and patriarchal order and rewrite an alternative televisual order. Burns-Ardolino argues that "female foursome shows" "depict a panoply of perspectives and positionalities that invite viewers to engage in resistant, negotiated and/or oppositional readings of mainstream, dominant culture" (2016, 1). It is the multiplicity and

---

3. "The possibilities of gender transformation are to be found . . . in the possibility of a different sort of repeating, in the breaking or subversive repetition of that style" (Butler 1988, 519–20).

multiformity of character positionalities of these women-ensemble-cast shows that multiply resistance to dominant culture. Moreover, it is also the accumulation of various chick TV antiheroines under an intertextual reading that further multiplies resistance—so much so that it becomes a new televisual order.

Arguably, all men characters intertextualize as well, especially antiheroes, as they possess certain characteristics that refer to various historical masculinities. However, since men have played the majority of hegemonic protagonists in the history of art in general and in television specifically—and women have mostly comprised minor, supportive roles (Faludi 1991; Brunsdon 2000)—the marginalized stars of chick TV intertextualize more specifically than do men's characters. Chick TV antiheroines' intertextuality references very particular, albeit proliferating, performances of femininity, mostly pertaining to digressions along the antiheroinist continua—the domestic, the sexual, the intellectual, and the classist.[4] Ironically, it is the long history of the stereotypical representation of women that allows for a specific thread of intertextuality and consequent intertextual resistance.

A perception of chick TV antiheroines as integrally intertextualizing creates a system of antiheroinisms that places singular feminist resistances in a broader context that sheds light on the systematic oppressions to which they resist. By the force of the fundamental intertextuality of antiheroine chick TV—that is, that characterizing a woman character as an antiheroine induces intertextuality with other antiheroines—each antiheroine's feminist resistance ceases to be a personal struggle and becomes a part of a collective struggle against hegemonic order. Intertextual reading of the repetitions of antiheroinisms across chick TV thus forms a sisterhood of resistances that not only exposes the systematic binds of the dominant order but also has the power to rewrite an alternative order.

---

4. See, for example, Burns-Ardolino (2016) on the formulas and stereotypes repeating in the representation of women on television, apotheosized in shows that feature foursomes.

In this way, reading antiheroine-chick TV intertextually is in itself a work of feminist resistance that renders the web of intertextualizing antiheroines into a system of feminist disruption to hegemonic order. In writing about *Ally McBeal*, Martha Nochimson notes that the show's "feminism was located not in Ally, but between characters, in new relational paradigms" (2000, 29). Such relational paradigms started to bud in chick TV of the late 1990s, with some shows ensemble-oriented and some protagonist-focused but all de facto exploring several women and their relationships. Shows such as *Ally McBeal* (1997–2002), *Sex and the City* (1998–2004), *Judging Amy* (1999–2005), *Providence* (1999–2002), *Gilmore Girls* (2000–2007), all of which have continued to run into the early 2000s, have become staple components of early twenty-first-century chick TV. The era's television dominance of relationships between women echoes contemporary politics of "third-wave feminism," which stands for fragmentation of interests, eschewing one essential feminist narrative or ideology in favor of a plurality of feminist voices (Walker 1995). The relational paradigms in chick TV series and between chick TV series (via intertextual repetition) form a web of resistance joined by their common ground to resist order.

In this chapter, I demonstrate the ways in which intertextual repetition of antiheroines' vilification marks a return to conservative gender representation on the one hand but offers space for transformation with each repetition on the other hand. Intertextuality of feminist resistances thus harnesses repetition to transform tradition rather than perpetuate it. As I address the feminist potential of transformation through intertextual repetition, I focus on the power of intertextuality to weave ties between antiheroines in a way that challenges chrononormativity and rewrites order.

Problematizing Intertextuality: Feminine Performance and Televisual Disorder

While the first three chapters dealt with temporal constructs in and of series (intradiegetic, episodic, and serial), this final chapter looks at temporal constructs between series, that is, intertextual. This most expansive layer of temporality ties together the tropes studied throughout to investigate more closely chick TV as a genre, albeit one the boundaries of which are permeable and changing. Analyses in the previous chapters focused on the refusing antiheroine—she who refuses to adhere to the demands of feminine performance as a domestic, maternal, sexually objectified, ladylike, wise heroinist woman. Significantly, these women's intertextual resistance to order both undermines hegemonic order (Zanger 2006) and creates a bond between them, like protesters fighting for the same cause. The case studies chosen for this chapter, however, focus on the other end of the antiheroinist continua—not the antiheroine who refuses feminine performance but the antiheroine who "overdoes" feminine performance.

The focus on the antiheroine who "overdoes" femininity serves to demonstrate the constructedness and elusiveness of gender performance. As discussed previously, "overdoing" femininity is as denigrated as "underdoing" it, and both performances—neither of which is "just right"—therefore bear resistant potential as they divert from order, thus exposing the arbitrariness and constructedness of feminine performance. As Mary Ann Doane suggests, the concept of the masquerade, which refers to excess performance of femininity, is read as a "destabilization" of the image of the feminine and a "defamiliarization of female iconography" (1982, 82). Both forms of diversion from the perceived proper amount of feminine performance—rejection of feminine performance and exaggeration of it—are considered a diversion from order and therefore signify a form of resistance. Hence, case studies in this chapter focus on the excessive extreme of the domestic and sexual continua—the women who "overdo" their femininity by immersing themselves in sexuality (labeled "promiscuous" or "slut") or domesticity (labeled subservient or "uptight").[5] *Desperate House-*

---

5. Kathleen Rowe examines the resistant and unruly force of the character of Roseanne (*Roseanne*) as such that constantly oscillates between the extremities, noting she is "a fat woman who is also sexual; a sloppy housewife who's a good mother: a 'loose' woman who is also tidy, who hates matrimony but loves her husband, who hates the ideology of 'true womanhood' yet considers herself a domestic goddess"

wives serves as the chapter's central case study with comparative analyses of intertextual repetitions of the "too sexual" antiheroine and the "too domestic" antiheroine.

Desperate Housewives: Rewriting Order via Intertextuality

Desperate Housewives is an ensemble show featuring four suburban wives who struggle with motherhood, marriage, career, status, and friendships. Generically soapy in its emphasis on women's issues and desires, talks and friendships, the series is one of the more quintessential examples of chick TV in this book. Although it amalgamates dark and comic undertones, it is predominantly dramatic, as it is consciously "empathetic to the dilemmas and difficulties of contemporary women" (Coward 2006). Consequently, *Desperate Housewives* presents an array of women characters, main and minor, along the spectrum of both sexual and domestic extremes as they intertextualize with contemporaneous and historical "excessive" performances of femininity.[6]

Sexual Overperformance: Desperate Housewives and Intertextuality of "Desperation"

Interestingly, many 2000s televisual antiheroines engage in sexual activity when viewers first encounter them, often casual (not part of a monogamous relationship) or extramarital sex. *Nurse Jackie*'s Jackie Peyton is seen sleeping with a coworker, though she is married to someone else, in the series pilot; *Desperate Housewives*' married Gabrielle Solis is featured sleeping with her gardener in the pilot episode; the pilot episode of *Transparent* finds Sarah Pfefferman sleeping with

---

(Rowe 1997, 91). By fluctuating between the extremes and not adhering to one coherent characterization as feminine, Roseanne thus exposes the ideology that lies beneath the social construct that is femininity.

6. Significantly, *Desperate Housewives* also features antiheroines who reject feminine performance along the various antiheroinist continua and not only such who "overdo" it.

a woman, though both of them are married to other people; *Being Mary Jane*'s pilot features the single Mary Jane Paul sleeping with a man she later realizes is married (and continues to sleep with him); *Grey's Anatomy*'s pilot portrays Meredith Grey having a one-night stand with a man she later realizes is married; *Six Feet Under*'s pilot reveals Brenda Chenowith having sex with a man she just met; and *Girls*' Hannah Horvath is engaged in sex with a nonexclusive partner (though she would like him to be) in the series pilot. Introducing women characters engaging in casual or adulterous sex (that is, sex that is not for the purpose of starting a family) is featured across networks and channels on both broadcast network shows (such as *Grey's Anatomy* and *Desperate Housewives* on ABC), which are held to greater censorship, and cable shows (such as *Six Feet Under* and *Girls* on HBO). Though cable shows are expected to be racier, it seems that the sexually active woman who is not family-oriented is a ubiquitous feature in early twenty-first-century US television.[7]

By initially presenting these women as they engage in "nonreproductive" (Halberstam 2011) sex, the texts in fact mark the women as resistant (Zanger 2006), antiheroinizing them in their refusal to adhere to social demands regarding women's sexual propriety.[8] The social double standard wherein women's sexual desires and conduct are considered lewd and men's commendable (Attwood 2007) is continuously reflected in cultural texts. Correspondingly, as per television characters, whereas men's extramarital sex is considered a sidestep

---

7. This representational trope is evident in other texts as well and seems to continue into the late 2010s. To name a few examples, the pilot of *Better Things* (2016–) captures Sam Fox contacting a man with whom it is clear she had a sexual relationship and who is unavailable; *Smilf* (2017–19) protagonist Bridgette Bird meets an old sexual partner in the series pilot, and though their sexual encounter is interrupted, it launches Bridgette's narrative; *Mrs. Fletcher* (2019) is mostly dedicated to the sexual awakening of empty-nester, single mom protagonist Eve Fletcher, and the pilot episode sees her seeking pleasure through pornography; and *Shrill* (2019–) features protagonist Annie sleeping with a casual partner (later realizing she is pregnant).

8. In *The Queer Art of Failure*, Halberstam posits "nonreproductive life styles" as "counterhegemonic" (2011, 89).

that does not necessarily interfere with their perpetuation of the symbolic order (though frequently adulterous, Tony Soprano is still very much a family man), women who choose to engage in sexual behavior that does not necessarily lead to family construction (including multiple sexual partners, uncommitted relationships, or infidelity) signify a disruption to order. Thus, the introduction of a woman character as nonreproductively sexual, that is, as someone who interrupts the chrononormative time flow that perpetuates familial order, is in fact a characterization technique of antiheroinization.[9] By utilizing this antiheroinization, chick TV series intertextualize with each other to challenge chrononormativity and rewrite an alternative order.

The "over" sexual woman is presented in chick TV in a way that both repeats tropes of sexual women in culture and transforms these tropes. These sexual women are presented committing sexual transgressions in varying degrees, spanning from sexual conduct that is explicitly framed as betrayal or sin to such that stems from desperation or liberation. I divide this spectrum into three categories: married women who pursue partners who are not their spouses, single women who pursue married partners, and single women who pursue multiple sexual partners. By looking at chick TV antiheroines through their "excessive" sexuality, I focus on the intertextual repetitions between "over" sexual antiheroines to detect the resistant force of the characterization technique and also of the text itself—the chick TV text that exhibits reflexive awareness of the history of the representation of sexual women. With this awareness, chick TV does not merely repeat conservative characterizations of sexual women but transforms them.

Gabrielle and Jackie: Unfaithful Married Women. The first subcategory of women who engage in nonreproductive sexual activity is married women who sleep with partners who are not their spouses. This category seemingly signifies an especially objectionable practice as the

---

9. Zanger perceives a woman's expression of sexuality as "a pocket of resistance" against the "sexual order" (2006, 122).

antiheroine's sexual excess is performed with full awareness of her boundary-crossing; she knowingly breaks a vow she has made. The characterization of unfaithful wives weaves intertextual ties to many cultural texts, from literature (such as *Anna Karenina*, written by Leo Tolstoy in 1878) to film (such as *Dial M for Murder*, directed by Alfred Hitchcock 1954, or *Body Heat*, directed by Lawrence Kasdan 1981), each of which features deceitful women whose villainy is expressed in their sexuality. These women are also typically "punished" by the text for their "excessive" sexuality and suffer various forms of retribution (Mulvey 1999 [1975]). Nevertheless, the intertextual repetitions of these twenty-first-century chick TV antiheroines transform the conservative paradigm of sexually unfaithful wives by reflexive awareness of the trope. This form of intertextuality thus repeats traditional narrative tropes in order to invert them, expose their constructedness, and deconstruct them, thereby drawing identification for the adulterous villainess and antiheroinizing her.

This intertextual reflexivity is evident in the case of the character of Gabrielle Solis, one of the four main characters of *Desperate Housewives*. She is depicted cheating on her husband in the series pilot, ostensibly repeating the characterization of the adulterous wife. However, her nonreproductive sexual choices are represented in a complex and ambivalent manner. When viewers are presented with Gabrielle's indiscretion, a dialogue with her lover unfolds her point of view. Gabrielle tells her lover that though her husband "promised to give me everything I've ever wanted" and in fact, she confesses, did, she is unfaithful to him primarily because she realized she "wanted all the wrong things," and, secondly, "because I don't want to wake up one morning with the sudden urge to blow my brains out." Gabrielle thus confesses to be having an affair so as to prevent herself from desperation-inspired suicidal behavior after her neighbor killed herself for no apparent reason.[10]

10. The show's pilot episode raises a powerful hypothesis, which harkens to the *Feminine Mystique* (Friedan 1970 [1963]), in its insinuation that the despair of suburban domesticity and the demands of homemaking and motherhood were what

In contrast, Edie Britt, one of the residents in the series' suburb, is often criticized by her neighbors and demonized by narration for her nonreproductive sexual choices. "Edie Britt was the most predatory divorcee in a five-block radius," the narrator reports when introducing Edie, adding that "her conquests were numerous, varied, and legendary." When the plot features a romantic rivalry between Edie and Susan Mayer, one of the series main characters who is a monogamous, not "too sexual" romantic heroine, the narrator frames the rivalry in saying that "Susan has met the enemy, and she was a slut" (pilot). The difference between the characterization of Edie and Gabrielle is thus focalization—the audience learns to sympathize with Gabrielle despite her transgressions because her inner motives and complex emotions are exposed, whereas Edie's motivations remain undisclosed, thus distancing identification and allowing for vilification. The way in which Gabrielle's infidelity is framed in the episode is what defines her as an antiheroine as the series creates a distinct divide between villainess and antiheroine by the text's tone toward each character's sexuality.

Thus, *Desperate Housewives* offers three sexual categories for women—the woman who practices sex for love (focalized, heroinized Susan), the sexual woman who seeks sex for the sake of sex (distanced, villainized Edie), and the woman who has sex not for love or family, but with whom the text draws identification (antiheroinized Gabrielle). The series thus portrays social perceptions regarding women's sexuality via two stereotypical extremes along the sexual continuum—the "Madonna" and the "whore"—and one more complex, transgressive but sympathetic character. In reading the series intertextually, the three characters stand in line with repetitions of sexual women in a way that enables a new option in between the "over" sexual villainess and she whose sexuality is "just right"—the antiheroine. Whereas Edie Britt is reprimanded by the text (it is in the narration), Gabrielle

---

drove the characters' housewife neighbor to suicide. However, the episode quickly abandoned that hypothesis when it turned out that she killed herself for fear that a secret she was keeping would be revealed.

is given no derogatory address despite her depicted cheating on her husband.

The text's identification with Gabrielle's point of view is further complicated by her identity as a Latinx, seeing as Latinx women are often hypersexualized and exotified (Molina Guzmán and Valdivia 2004). Characterizing Gabrielle through sexual subjectivity instead of sexually objectifying her or castigating her for her sexuality effectively rewrites traditional narrative order. By having the character of Edie intertextually repeat the stereotype of the villainous sexual woman, *Desperate Housewives*' further repetition of the woman who expresses "excessive" sexuality—Gabrielle—does not villainize her but antiheroinizes her, thus rewriting traditional narrative order. Interestingly, the initially vilified character of Edie Britt undergoes a process of humanization and multilayering throughout the series, shifting away from villainessness and closer to antiheroinism by way of transformative repetition.

A contemporaneous intertextual antiheroine, *Nurse Jackie*'s protagonist, is, like Gabrielle, presented as adulterous as early as in the pilot episode. However, if Gabrielle's transgression is designed to draw empathy, Jackie's is certainly not designed for empathy's sake. In fact, in Jackie's case, viewers first learn about her lover, and only later, at the end of the episode, discover Jackie is married to someone else. The revelation of her domestic life comes as a surprise as she enters her house toward the end of the episode, takes a wedding band out of her pocket, puts it on her finger, and walks into the kitchen, where her husband awaits. Though Jackie's motives and emotions are not unfolded, she is not villainized as is *Desperate Housewives*' Edie because she inhabits both villainess traits, with no justification for infidelity, as well as heroic traits, with cheating with a man she indeed loves.

The encompassing of both villainessness and heroism complicates Jackie's motives, as she loves both the man to whom she is married and the man with whom she cheats but lies to both. The possession of both characterizational extremities in the character of Jackie fits Buonanno's perception of antiheroinism as liminality between good and bad, between conforming to social demands and defying them (Buonanno 2017, 12). Jackie's intertextualization with parallel instances of women's sexual expression, such as Gabrielle's, and not only with past representations of adulterous villainesses who are punished for their sexual pursuits, works both to antiheroinize her and to bolster her contemporaneous web of antiheroines, thus forcefully disrupting the stronghold of patriarchal representational power. By positioning Jackie vis-à-vis her intertextual antiheroines, her antiheroinism becomes a struggle to design subjectivity in the face of social demands rather than an isolated case of one woman's vilified sexual transgression.

Meredith and Mary Jane: Single Women Sleeping with Married Men. The second subcategory of women who engage in nonreproductive sex is women who sleep with married men. I focus on two such women: *Grey's Anatomy*'s Meredith and *Being Mary Jane*'s Mary Jane, both of whom sleep with men casually and later find out these men are married. Seeing as both these women are lead characters with whom viewers are expected to identify, the late revelation of the men's marital status works to both relieve the women of any premeditated wrongdoing—assuming that had they known these men are married they may not have gone into a sexual relationship with them—and to place the blame on the men, who are both knowingly committing adultery and keeping the information of their status secret from their partners.

Comparing this category to the previous one, it becomes evident that women who cheat on their husbands are still capable of becoming identifiable characters (Gabrielle, Jackie), whereas single women who (knowingly) cheat with married men are well beyond the boundaries of identification (Edie). However, to complicate this category further, though both Meredith and Mary Jane do not know their sexual partners are married on their respective pilot episodes—ostensibly absolving them of malicious intent and therefore allowing identification—later in the series, both continue to sleep with their respective married lovers, at which point the women do know of the men's marital status. Nevertheless, here too, as in the previous category, focalizing the adulterous antiheroine and revealing her complex and romantic motives maintains identification, as the texts construct Meredith and Mary Jane as sympathetic, making their adultery as driven either by unawareness or by love and their promiscuity as an escape from the despair of unrequited love.[11]

The drawing of and pushing back against identification defines the women's antiheroinism (Nussbaum 2013b), a mechanism that is employed through intertextual repetition of representations of adulterous women, both coeval, as in *Desperate Housewives*, and past representations of women sexual transgressors in film and television—from *I'm No Angel*'s Tira (1933), *Gilda*'s Gilda (1946), *Fatal Attraction*'s Alex Forrest (1987), and *Basic Instinct*'s Catherine Tramell (1992), to *Golden Girls*' Blanche Devereaux (1985–92), *Sex and the City*'s Samantha Jones (1998–2004), or *Broad City*'s Ilana Wexler (2014–19). By intertextually repeating the trope of the single woman who sleeps with a married man, *Grey's Anatomy* and *Being Mary Jane* set the stage for the narrative expectation of punishment. By maintaining the liminal complexity of the women's moral and gendered characterization, however, the texts play with the anticipation of retribution, as the women are not traditionally punished and manage to find love and contentment despite many tribulations along the way.[12] By intertextually repeating the trope of the temptress woman who sleeps with

---

11. That Meredith is motivated by love may be read as a testament to the text's conservativism rather than its subversion. Knisely notes that "the positive depiction of Meredith's drunken promiscuity is arguably dependent upon her longstanding quest for her fantasy 'Mr. Right' who she finds in Derek," thus asking, "Could we see Meredith's behavior as acceptable if her drunken promiscuity was an end in itself?" (2008, 124). In reference to intertextual ties, however, Meredith's sexuality is depicted as complex and not demonized. Further intertextual repetitions of sexual women in chick TV portray women's sexuality for its own sake, as elaborated in the next section.

12. At some point during *Grey's Anatomy*, Derek—Meredith's once married lover and later husband and father of her three children—dies (season 11, episode 21, "How to Save a Life"). This event is extratextually driven by the resignation of Patrick Dempsey, the actor who plays Derek in the show, and is therefore not a classical narrative "punishment" for the fact that the marriage was initiated by infidelity.

a married man—this time giving her voice and agency—transformation occurs. By attributing identification to sexual women, the text antiheroinizes them rather than villainizes them, thus engendering an alternative narrative order.

Antiheroinization through intertextual repetition is exemplified in *Being Mary Jane*'s first season's third episode ("The Huxtables Have Fallen"), in which Mary Jane's frustration about her romantic situation is echoed by radio shows. Disappointed after another failed encounter in which a disingenuous marriage proposal is offered from the married man with whom she has been sleeping, Mary Jane steps into her car and turns on the radio. "All men don't cheat," a woman's voice utters. "Although I think there's a higher rate of it than is ever reported. Yes, it's true that nature designed us to procreate—" When Mary Jane changes the station, a man's voice pronounces, "the Word tells us that husbands are designed to love their wives as Christ loves—" A third switch of station lands on a hip-hop song that notes, "It's kinda hard to do your thing when everyone's surrounding . . . everybody step back—"[13]

The three stations encapsulate Mary Jane's possible choices for her next move. She could either take the cynical route, that which leans on biological determinism; she could take the route of faith, that which leans on religious determinism; or she could choose not to choose, to have others "step back" and let her "do [her] thing." The song continues into the following scene, in which Mary Jane is captured moving to the music. She has therefore chosen her path. She would not be counting on a man whose love for his wife is tantamount to that of Jesus Christ—an attitude that could be compared to the heroinist, *Desperate Housewives*' Susan's sex-for-love attitude, which Mary Jane thought she was promoting with her lover. She would also not assume that every man is a cheater as was her lover—an attitude that goes by

---

Still, if reviewed textually, in exclusion from contextual circumstances, his death arrives much later in the show (11 seasons after the two met).

13. The song is titled "Swing," by hip hop artist Savage (Demetrius Savelio), from his 2005 album *Moonshine*.

way of the villainous trajectory of manipulative and exploitative sexual conduct, as is attributed to *Desperate Housewives*' Edie. Instead, Mary Jane relinquishes the dichotomous belief system by which sex is a manifestation of either love or manipulation and allows herself to "do [her] thing," that is, allow herself to express desire, including sexual desire. Mary Jane's sexual choices thus reflect her antiheroinism, designed in reference to her intertextual ties, as she attempts to negotiate her (sexual) subjectivity.

It is important to note that as a Black woman, Mary Jane struggles with stereotypes that involve race as well as gender. More specifically, the character of a sexual Black woman would be read in reference to the "Jezebel stereotype" (West 2012, 294). The perception of Black women as sexual in American culture spans from the "Hottentot Venus," the objectified and sexualized image of a Black woman in the nineteenth century (Gilman 1985), and the antebellum "Jezebel stereotype, which branded Black women as sexually promiscuous and immoral" (and thereby "could not be rape victims because they always desired sex" [West 2012, 294]), to the more submissive images of Black women (versus white women) in pornography (Hill Collins 2005, 137), and the contemporary "'hoochies,' 'freaks,' 'hoodrats,' or 'chickenheads'" (West 294). Indeed, all characterizations of women inevitably resonate with the charged Madonna/whore dichotomy, but stereotypes of Black women (sexual and others) have been more dehumanizing than the stereotypes that burden white women (Hill Collins 2005; Warner 2015). Furthermore, the intersectional identity of the Black woman, stereotyped and objectified in the juncture of both race and gender, positions Mary Jane's sexuality as improper in a manner that is embedded in the traditional objectification of Black women.

Both *Grey's Anatomy* and *Being Mary Jane* express awareness of televisual tropes and motifs regarding women and their sexuality. The shows feature diegetic criticism aimed at Meredith (she refers to herself as "adulterous whore" and "dirty mistress") and Mary Jane (noted "homewrecker"), thereby reflecting social criticism directed at single women who, more often than not, are blamed for infidelity much more so than are the married men with whom they cheat. This awareness of the ways in which women's sexual expressions are perceived socially and represented culturally places the series in tacit intertextuality with each other and with other parallel and past representations of sexual women who were punished for their sexuality (femme fatales, vamps, jezebels, and temptresses of cultural history). In portraying women's nonreproductive sexual desire with its attached social criticism, the series exhibit awareness of the tradition of villainizing sexual women. By attaching these traditionally vilified features to their identifiable protagonists, the texts defuse the habitually negative perception of women's sexuality, positioning these women in antiheroinism and thus rewriting narrative and social order.

Brenda and Hannah: Multiple Nonmonogamous Relationships. Whereas the examples above address sexual conduct that is discredited across gender lines—both men and women who engage in infidelity are socially criticized (arguably, women more harshly)—the social category of "promiscuity" is very much gendered. The third subcategory of women who engage in nonreproductive sexual activity consists of women who are single but whose sexual lives are "excessive." This category is the most fraught, as it emphasizes the constructedness of feminine performance with regard to sexuality: what is the "right" amount of sexual desire? What is the "right" number of sexual partners? This is obviously a discursive category meant to police women's bodies, and many twenty-first-century chick TV representations express in their narratives a reflexive awareness of the gendered aspects of sexuality and the constructed nature of its social and cultural perceptions. By intertextually repeating representations of "over" sexual women, chick TV texts in the 2000s offer a metatextual critique of the "punitive classification of female sexuality" (Hanson and O'Rawe 2010, 3), as can be seen in the following examples.

Brenda Chenowith, one of the main characters of *Six Feet Under*, is characterized by her sexuality as early as the pilot episode of the series. In the episode, she sleeps with Nate Fisher, the eldest son of the family on which the series centers. Having just met her sexual partner, Brenda confesses to having never done "this" before, namely, sleeping with someone she has just met, but later in the episode, she casually states she was lying. This duality positions Brenda as a sexual woman who is at the same time aware of the social vilification of sexual women, thereby attempting to characterize herself as usually more vigilant when it comes to sexual encounters. The pilot thus launches a sexual characterization of Brenda, as, during *Six Feet Under*'s five seasons, she has many sexual encounters, some with strangers, some with multiple partners, some for money, some while she is engaged, some while in a program for sex addicts. In all these instances, her sexual conduct is interwoven with her decisions regarding family, self, relationships, and other features that define her character.[14] Merry Lisa Johnson sees Brenda's sexual encounters as a "complex . . . mixture of freedom and neurosis" set to negotiate the boundaries of her subjectivity (2004, 31–32). Indeed, her sexual encounters are often the result of power dynamics with her partners—her commitment to Nate drives her to question her choices and cheat; her relationship with Joe starts with abstinence and ends with sexual domination games—or with herself and her desire for a family versus her desire for emotional and sexual autonomy.

Such characterization is echoed in Seel's perception of antiheroinism, which focuses on the antiheroine's negotiation of her identity between social and patriarchal prescriptions and her desire for autonomy and subjectivity (2006, 126). The depiction of Brenda's sexuality, which serves as a characterization technique to antiheroinize her, is part of *Six Feet Under*'s textual "awareness" of the history of the representation of women's sexuality. The tradition of chastising women for expressing their sexuality is heavily embedded in western culture (Zanger 2006, 122) as far back as Potiphar's Wife and Aphrodite. The convention of penalizing women for promiscuity is longstanding, from social punishment depicted in Nathaniel Hawthorne's *The Scarlet Letter* in 1850 to self-inflicted punishment in Gustave Flaubert's

---

14. Brenda "consistently identifies and then violates borders . . . struggles . . . to develop specific frameworks for challenging patriarchal borders and gendered boundaries" (MacLeod 2005, 136).

Madame Bovary in 1856 and Leo Tolstoy's *Anna Karenina* in 1878 to more symbolic forms of punishment regarding sexuality and femininity, such as murder by vengeful sexual partners, as in Richard Brooks's 1977 film *Looking for Mr. Goodbar*; miscarriage, as in Adrian Lyne's 1987 film *Fatal Attraction*; rape, as in Lars von Trier's 2013 film *Nymphomaniac*; or a sexually transmitted disease, as in Tyler Perry's 2013 film *Temptation: Confessions of a Marriage Counselor*.

Twenty-first-century chick TV texts—such as *Grey's Anatomy*, *Being Mary Jane*, and *Six Feet Under*—which characterize sexual women in a way that is aware of the trope's stereotypical lineage, repeat the trope in a way that sheds light on the oppressive contexts around the women rather than framing the women themselves as "sinners." Examples of texts that address the social penalization of sexual women can be seen in twentieth-century television, with examples being *Golden Girls*' (1985–92) Blanche Deveraux and *Sex and the City*'s (1998–2004) Samantha Jones. However, it is the twenty-first century that introduced a web of texts that exhibit awareness of the narrative tradition of the "punitive classification of female sexuality" (Hanson and O'Rawe 2010, 3), by which even if a narrative features women's sexuality, "before the curtain falls, sexual order must be restored" (Zanger 2006, 122). Twenty-first-century chick TV often exhibits reflexive awareness of these traditions in ways that expose the social bias against women's sexuality and the systematic perpetuation of this bias in cultural representations, as can be seen in the awareness of Meredith and Mary Jane to their narrative roles as "adulteresses" or "homewreckers."

Six Feet Under presents a scene that illustrates such awareness of and reference to the way women's sexuality is represented when Brenda imagines a fraught conversation with the spirit of Lisa, her soon-to-be-husband's dead wife.[15] On her wedding day, soon after having had

---

15. This convention is very common in *Six Feet Under*. As a series that revolves around death with its main ensemble a family that runs a funeral home, almost every episode of *Six Feet Under* presents a character of a dead person that "talks" with one of the main characters. This convention does not step into genres of fantasy but

a miscarriage, Brenda processes her mixed feelings about her sexuality by imagining an argument with the late Lisa:

> LISA: You don't have to worry about it being like my wedding. I had a three-month-old baby when I got married, so it was a much happier event, obviously. It all came very easy to me . . . but I was always maternal.
> BRENDA: I'm fucking maternal.
> LISA: Oh, come on, I mean, look at your past. You're a slutbag. You were.
> BRENDA: That's got nothing to do with it.
> LISA: Of course it does. All the moments of your life have led to this one. You're being punished.
> BRENDA: I don't believe in that.
> LISA: Your insides must have gotten damaged from all that anonymous cock. Oh, come on. That's why this happened to you. . . . Every time you try to have a nice normal life, you fuck it up. You're never going to have your little Happily-Ever-After moment, no matter how many white veils you put on, honey. You're just too fucked up for all that. Maybe you should just accept that instead of trying to be something you're not.
> ("A Coat of White Primer" 5.1)

Seeing as Lisa's words are a manifestation of Brenda's psyche, it is clear that Brenda is well aware of the cultural cliché of a sexual woman becoming a cautionary tale against "promiscuity." Nevertheless, and though she expresses disbelief at the idea that she is being punished, Brenda seems insecure about her choices, insecurity that is manifested both in Lisa's words and in Brenda's apprehensive protests.

Though Brenda is ambivalent, the text itself takes a stand. By presenting awareness of the miscarriage-as-punishment-for-promiscuity narrative, *Six Feet Under* uses implicit intertextuality to other characters of sexual women, conjuring those who were punished by their

---

is framed as a realistic manifestation of the characters' imagination, with the dead symbolizing the characters' critical superegos.

narratives for their sexuality, intertextually repeating their tales in order to transform them. The text thus intertextually repeats the miscarriage-as-punishment-for-promiscuity narrative but then harnesses it to bring about a different narrative order. Brenda's miscarriage narrative works to deconstruct the cultural tradition that polices women's sexuality since she goes on to have the family she wants, midway obstacles notwithstanding. By absorbing its intertextual references, the text sheds light on western culture's systematic policing of women's sexual desires and subjectivities, thus paving the way for characters' antiheroinist resistance to such policing.

The sexual women of twenty-first-century US chick TV are antiheroinized via intertextuality, "acquiring subjectivity" by "playing with a media lexicon of cultural identities, exposing clichés, challenging gendered expectations" (McCabe writes this about Claire in *Six Feet Under* [2005, 128–29]). The texts of twenty-first-century chick TV have subsumed the knowledge of the history of the representation of sexual women. If sexual women characters until the early twentieth century were often punished for their sexuality, as in the case of fallen women or femme fatales, then late twentieth-century representations leaned toward more sexually liberated women, with second-wave feminism's sexual revolution manifested in *Mary Tyler Moore Show*'s insinuation that its lead character was using birth control pills and thus implying she was having extramarital sex, *Maude*'s (1972–78) depiction of a character undergoing an abortion, and *Golden Girls* presenting unabashed sexuality. Turn of the century representations were more explicit about women's sexuality, a trend epitomized in *Sex and the City* openly discussing women's sexual desires and practices. Ultimately, and in keeping with third-wave sensibility, twenty-first-century representations of sexual women are not only explicit about women's diverse sexualities but also about the representation of women's sexualities, thus offering metatextual commentary that intertextually ties televisual sexual women.[16]

---

16. Susan Wolfe and Lee Ann Roripaugh identify metatextual narratives on *The L Word*—metatextuality which "reflects the inherent difficulty of representing

As in the case of *Six Feet Under*'s scene that does not offer judgment of Brenda's sexuality but presents the existence of such social judgment only to disclaim it, *Girls* bases its discourse of sexuality on a repetition of and resistance to intertextual sexualities. For example, when Hannah realizes she contracted a sexually transmitted disease, the text both frames the STD as "punishment" for her uncommitted sexual life (Hannah is frightened and guilty, her friend Marnie sobs), and celebrates it ("All Adventurous Women Do," the title of the episode, is a sentence uttered several times during the episode to signify that an STD is a symbol of adventurousness). Thus, "All Adventurous Women Do" (season 1, episode 3) shifts between the tragic and the romantic, positioning Hannah via intertextuality with both the sexual villainesses of puritanism and the sexual heroines of feminist liberation, thereby characterizing her as a sexual antiheroine whose sexuality is complex, both liberating and straining, and constantly negotiated.

Instead of portraying sexual women as fallen on the one hand or as liberated on the other, chick TV series in the 2000s exhibit complexities regarding sex, as can be seen in Hannah's joys and sorrows, Brenda's independence and regret, or Mary Jane's romanticism and lamentations. The sexual women of twenty-first-century chick TV are characterized by intertextual repetition as the antiheroinist complexities that define them are both derived from representations of the past—to which the texts are aware and with which they play—and connect to coeval representations, themselves aware of textual traditions, conventions, and stereotypes. Indeed, an examination of the representation of twenty-first-century chick TV women's sexuality, more specifically sexuality that involves women's desires, pleasures, and subjectivities rather than leading to reproduction or objectification, reveals an attempt to offer an alternative narrative order, one which repeats in order to transform.

---

lesbians (or any women) on the screen because female characters are always open to exploitative readings" (2006, 53).

As the sexual continuum is a critical feature of feminine performance, both of its extremes are governed by social regulations against which antiheroines are characterized—excessive performance of sexuality is as regulated and antiheroinizing as is a refusal of its performance. Another dominant form of representation of the demands of femininity and their potential resistances, one no less politically fraught than sexuality, is the social and cultural category of domesticity, the intertextual repetitions of which are discussed next with a focus on the potential of such to rewrite order.

Domestic Overperformance: Desperate Housewives
and Intertextuality of Housewifery

On the other end of the feminine "overperformance" spectrum lies the woman whose excess is related to her domesticity. She is the woman who takes her domestic and familial obligations "too far," according to the delicate and precarious, ever-changing equilibrium that determines the coordinates of feminine performance. If the "oversexual" antiheroine assumes her social role of a sexualized object but problematizes it so as to become a sexual subject by following her own desire rather than the desire of others, then the "overdomestic" antiheroine problematizes the social demand that women be domestic by "owning" her own domesticity. Instead of tending to the domestic and familial for the sake of others, the "overdomestic" antiheroine chooses domesticity that is concurred with her desire rather than with the desire of others. The following examples will demonstrate that even though she adheres to the demands of feminine performance in the form of domestic servitude, the woman character that exceeds social expectations of the proper measure of domestic investment is antiheroinized due to her diversion from and disruption to order. Furthermore, by intertextually repeating characteristics of "overinvestment" in domesticity, twenty-first-century chick TV transforms the devaluation of the "overdomestic" woman character by antiheroinizing her and rewriting order.

Unlike the performative excess of domestic women in the history of US film and television, the women of twenty-first-century chick TV, like the women who express sexual excess, are reflexive characters in texts that exhibit familiarity with discourses of domesticity. In the history of the representation of women in the household, being a homemaker was positioned as a successful form of feminine performance. "Fulfillment as a woman had only one definition for American women after 1949—the housewife-mother," Friedan famously noted (1970 [1963], 38). However, homemaking was not supposed to come at the expense of marital, parental, and other social commitments. Housewives too immersed in domestic work were mocked for knowing their way only around the home and nowhere else, from the humorous case of the character of Gracie Allen of *The George Burns and Gracie Allen Show* (1950–58), who is "constantly arranging flowers or making and serving coffee but not sense" (Mellencamp 1986, 83), to the horror-infused *Stepford Wives* (1975), in which the women who are entrenched in domesticity are represented as so dumb that the revelation that they are robots comes as no surprise.[17]

Though the ridicule of Gracie is rooted in masculine patronizing and the ridicule of the ladies of the town of Stepford is rooted in second-wave feminist criticism of the patriarchal demand that women tend to the household, in both cases the women who are immersed in housewifery are derided. Unlike the homemakers who were belittled in depictions that preceded the twenty-first century, the women who express domestic performative excess in twenty-first-century chick TV are infused with the knowledge of the conventions of representation—by which homemakers are dismissed as frivolous—and use this knowledge to break these conventions. For example, the character of Bree van de Kamp in *Desperate Housewives* who portrays the

---

17. Patricia Mellencamp focuses on the way in which, despite all these characteristics, Gracie manages to escape order and remains "out of (or beyond) men's control" (1986, 83). Nevertheless, the premise of the reading that exposes Gracie's disorder is based on the fact that she is mocked by the text as she who is making the home, but, and perhaps consequently, not sense.

"perfect housewife" so consumed with maintaining her home that she loses sight of everything else also encapsulates intertextual knowledge as her character is designed through its cultural references. Particularly, because she is compared both to villainized women who express "over investment in domesticity" (Sharp 2006, 125) on the one hand (her son likens her to the robotic homemakers of *Stepford Wives*) and to tales of domestic triumph on the other (her character indirectly references *Mildred Pierce* [1945] in utilizing her domestic skills in business), she escapes the dichotomy of either validated or ridiculed domestic woman as she constantly shifts between various perceptions of domesticity.[18]

The text itself seems ambivalent toward Bree's conduct, as her attraction to the domestic is often presented comically, as if to ridicule her excess, but when her family members criticize her for overimmersion in domesticity, the text turns to side with her. In the pilot episode, Bree's husband Rex, frustrated with his wife's image of the perfect housewife, scoffs her,

> I'm sick of you being so damn perfect all the time. . . . You're this plastic suburban housewife with her pearls and her spatula who says things like "we owe the Hendersons a dinner." Where's the woman I fell in love with, who used to burn the toast, and drink milk out of the carton, and laugh? I need her. Not this cold, perfect thing you've become. (pilot)

Though the tone of the scene initially induces empathy for the youthful man who misses his wife's human imperfections, it gradually frames the moment as one of an unfair, little-too-harsh piece of criticism. Soon after her husband concludes his lament, the camera follows Bree into the bathroom, where she cries. In the bathroom, the frame

---

18. The 1975 film *Stepford Wives* is based on a 1972 novel by the same name (Ira Levin, *Stepford Wives*) and was remade as more a comedy than a horror film in 2004 by Frank Oz. The film *Mildred Pierce* is based on a 1941 novel by the same name (James M. Cain 1941).

captures both Bree's back and her reflection in the mirror, creating identification with her image and humanizing the seemingly perfect housewife.

In a later episode, Bree attempts to regain her husband's affection by uncharacteristically seducing him with a display of sexualized performance, lingerie and sensual bravado included, thereby contradicting her usually prudish behavior. Bree's domestic persona trumps her sexual one, however, as she interrupts physical intimacy to stop a burrito her husband placed on the nightstand from spilling on the floor, exclaiming, after her husband expresses disappointment at her priorities, "Well, it's obvious you've never had to remove a cheese stain" (season 1, episode 6, "Running to Stand Still"). This comic endnote may be designed for laughs but is also framed as Bree's reclaiming of her own agency. She works hard at domesticity, and the text insists on letting it be known. Unlike *The George Burns and Gracie Allen Show*'s Gracie, who regains identification through her cooperation with being the butt of the joke and being fondly mocked for her ditzy behavior, Bree is very much aware of how she is perceived. She regains identification through her refusal to cooperate with being ridiculed. Both Bree herself and the text she occupies thus exhibit awareness of the tradition of the representation of the overdomestic housewife, as her characterization "lifts the lid on how patriarchy has long vilified the very ideal it celebrates" (McCabe 2006, 81).[19] Though Bree is initially characterized as overimmersed in domesticity, the text continuously pushes back against the long-established oversimplification of her character, thus antiheroinizing her.

A similar position is occupied by Christine Brown, one of the main characters of the docusoap *Sister Wives*, which follows a polygamist family consisting of one husband and four wives—Meri, Janelle, Christine, and Robyn. Possessing docusoap features, the series complies with chick TV categorization in its focus on women and their

---

19. McCabe adds that Bree's extremely well-executed performance of the "feminine ideal" sheds light on the issue of performance itself and its demands (2006, 75).

relationships with each other and others (mostly their husband and children), centralizing emotion and talk, family and marriage. As the polygamist Brown family grew over the years, the four wives have gradually followed different familial responsibilities, with each wife fulfilling a distinct stereotypical role for patriarch Kody. Meri, the first wife, mothers him, giving him an emotional bosom to embrace, making him feel needed (at least at first); Janelle, the second wife, serves as a major financial provider in the household and Kody's "best friend," with whom he can "talk about everything and anything" (season 1, episode 9, "Sister Wives Honeymoon Special"); Christine, the third wife, takes care of the children and home; and Robyn, though this is not explicitly addressed, is Kody's new and exciting lover, with whom he is most romantic.

Though she gravitated toward her domestic role willingly (as she explicates in the pilot episode of the series), Christine believes that immersion in homemaking is what lies beneath the fact that she "was never valued as an intellectual" by her husband (season 1, episode 9, "*Sister Wives* Honeymoon Special"). As is the fictional Bree, Christine is also well aware of how domestic women are perceived in culture, especially those who are "too domestic." Moreover, Christine fears she is perceived as dumb due to her preoccupation with domestic chores. The intertextuality of the woman who is "too domestic" for her own good thus crosses generic lines, with both real and fictional representations. Both *Desperate Housewives*' Bree and *Sister Wives*' Christine essentially cooperate with patriarchal order in fulfilling the domestic exigencies of feminine performance but feel unappreciated as they are not rewarded for their conformity.

Though the women who fulfill their gender roles are expected to thrive under social validation, both Bree and Christine are devalued because they perform their femininity too extremely and are perceived to be doing so at the expense of romantic or intellectual pursuits. In this way, Bree and Christine, though living under very different circumstances—the former a fictional WASP housewife and the latter a reality-TV polygamist wife—face similar issues regarding the struggle with feminine performance repeated across intertextual lines.

By reading Bree and Christine together, it becomes evident that both remain outside the lines of social validation for their overinvestment in domesticity as are the women who are judged for their underinvestment in domesticity, such as *Real Housewives*' Kenya who presents store-bought food as homemade, *Grey's Anatomy*'s Cristina who expresses aversion toward any domestic task, or *Six Feet Under*'s Claire who refuses to nest or nurse others.[20] The "too domestic" women thus effectively resist the policing of domestic feminine performance and are antiheroinized by their intertextual ties.

The characterizational mode of overinvestment in domesticity is also repeated in *Six Feet Under*'s Ruth Fisher, who married young, had children, and whose main occupation is as a housewife. Ruth is often seen in the house, cooking or cleaning. In fact, the series premiere first presents her as she is cooking. When she receives a phone call informing her that her husband has died, she collapses, throwing kitchenware around the room. When her son David enters the kitchen, alarmed by the clamor, she tells him, "Your father is dead. Your father is dead, and my pot roast is ruined" (1.1 pilot). Through this grief-stricken, verging on the grotesque response, *Six Feet Under* mocks Ruth's extreme commitment to domesticity, with the cynical equation of the disaster of her sudden widowhood to a ruined dinner.

However, as the series progresses, Ruth's character becomes more humanized and identifiable. Significantly, she becomes more identifiable without being stripped away from her domestic characterization. It is not as if she must abandon homemaking so as to obtain valued subjectivity, thereby perpetuating the role of housewife as inferior.

20. "I don't do laundry; I buy new underwear. . . . I don't wash dishes, vacuum, or put the toilet paper on the holder. I hired a maid once . . . she ran away crying. The only things in my fridge are water, vodka, and diet soda, and I don't care," *Grey's Anatomy*'s Cristina warns a boyfriend before moving in together (season 2, episode 10, "Much Too Much"). Relatedly, *Six Feet Under*'s Claire tells an ex-boyfriend, "I'm not some nurse who's here to take care of the misfits," when he asks her for support after breaking up with her (season 3, episode 10, "Everyone Leaves").

Thus, *Six Feet Under* repeats the narrative tradition of representing homemakers as ridiculously "too domestic" in order to invert it. By intertextually referencing the "excessive" housewife and humanizing her, *Six Feet Under* deconstructs the domestic performance of femininity, metatextually demonstrating that even those who perform femininity "too well" may be subject to criticism, thereby exposing the oppressive constructedness of femininity.

Ruth possesses a contradictory character, the contradictions of which are often related to her domestic overperformance. On the one hand, she admits to having chosen to be a wife and mother and to have never regretted that choice; on the other hand, she seems to express remorse for the losses she endured as a result of that choice. The inconsistency in her perception of her wifery and motherhood often appears, as it does in a conversation she has with her daughter Claire:

> RUTH: I never got to go to college.
> CLAIRE: Did you ever want to?
> RUTH: I did. I wanted to study French feminist writers.
> CLAIRE: You're a feminist, mom?
> RUTH: Feminism means being accepted for who you are. I wanted to be a wife and a mother. I never gave anything up to be a mother or a wife. It was what I wanted.
> CLAIRE: I thought you just said you gave up going to college.
> (season 2, episode 12, "I'll Take You")

Six Feet Under thus repeats the familiar trope of the sacrificial mother but rewrites it to establish Ruth's antiheroinist dual nature—she both mourns her sacrifices and has no regrets about her choices. Thus, Ruth antiheroinistically resists the traditional patronizing of women who are "too domestic" by insisting on her own complexities and multitudes.

Positioning *Six Feet Under*'s Ruth, *Desperate Housewives*' Bree, and *Sister Wives*' Christine parallel to each other emphasizes that whether one makes an effort to meet patriarchal demands and follow hegemonic order or opposes these demands and the order they serve, proper femininity is so elusive that one will never be able to perform it "just right." Chick TV intertextuality thus creates a web of antiheroines whose various forms of "failure" to adhere to patriarchal order stress that it is the order that is failing those who try to maintain it rather than the individuals who are the "failures." By intertextually repeating historical and contemporaneous representations of housewives and homemakers, domestic women characters of twenty-first-century chick TV are no longer superficially stereotyped; rather, they are antiheroinized through their resistance to adhere to the perceivable proper amount of investment in domesticity. Thus, repetition becomes rewriting.

The antiheroine-televisual web, constructed of the various representations of antiheroines, functions as "a passage, an overcrossing" (Barthes 1977, 159), an ontological bridge through which characters and themes repeat, intertextualize, transform each other, and join each other to rewrite order. Each text, therefore, can be read in and of itself and in relation to other texts. This allows each series to be read as a dual text, as it can promote certain perceptions within the confines of its own narrative but undermine the same perceptions or endorse different ones when read in correlation with its intertexts. This pertains, for example, to reading *Sister Wives'* Christine as a symbol of conservative feminine domesticity on its own (Jorgenson 2014) and as a resistance to the criticized overperformance of femininity intertextually. Ultimately, when read intertextually, antiheroines (both those who underdo feminine performance and those who overdo it) make up a cumulative web of resistances diverse enough to show that various routes taken by women to adapt to the elusive constraints of patriarchy have repeatedly fallen short, thereby exposing how confining and arbitrary feminine performance really is. More so than that, an intertextual reading of chick TV antiheroines offers a textual web vast enough to undermine and rewrite narrative and patriarchal order.

Textual Sisterhood: Intertextual Repetition as Transformative Antiheroinism

Jeremy Butler addresses resistant television women characters in noting that the women of *Designing Women* "belong to an unruly sisterhood of TV women who have disrupted the discourse of patriarchy, who have dared to become subjects in a medium and a culture that thrives on the objectification of women" (1993, 17). These women form a sisterhood of antiheroinist characters, repeating across various texts, with their resistance formulated by their intertextual ties to each other. Twenty-first-century chick TV antiheroines belong to this televisual sisterhood yet bear some differences from their older "sisters." First, as elaborated in previous chapters, 2000s chick TV antiheroinism is entwined with complex textual temporality that is characterized in conjunction with intradiegetic devices, flashes, the serial structure itself, or intertextual repetition. Second, twenty-first-century chick TV antiheroines function in cross-referential reflexivity as the texts they inhabit absorb previous and parallel representations of women and script themselves in awareness of the narrative traditions behind them.

Surely, reflexivity and intertextuality are not twenty-first-century inventions, nor are they televisual inventions. Still, I maintain that the narrative tradition of the marginalization and trivialization of women's stories has created a metatextual bond between women characters who resist order. Similarly, Kyra Hunting's "chick-lit television" category, which "responds to the evolving gender norms in American culture," is a category that "emphasizes dialogism" and intertextuality (2012, 188). Moreover, Hunting asserts, though single episodes of the series she analyzes (*Sex and the City*, *Lipstick Jungle*, and *The Cashmere Mafia*) may be perpetuating feminine stereotypes

> and may even appear regressive, when these series are read in relationship to each other, . . . they demonstrate that no matter how economically successful, traditionally beautiful, racially privileged

or . . . willing to submit to gender norms, it takes constant negotiation of institutional and cultural constraints for a woman to achieve a liberated and fulfilling life. (2012, 193)

In exposing the "constant negotiation" involved in gender norms, intertextual reading calls their normalization into question. It is not only the comparative value of antiheroinist intertextual repetition—as in serial reading—that promotes feminist resistance but also the cumulative value of antiheroinism amassed via intertextual repetition into an alternative narrative order.

Sister Wives, for example, other than having several of its characters intertextualize with other antiheroines in the twenty-first-century televisual landscape, intertextualizes with other shows that present a group of women that revolve around a single man, both scripted and nonscripted. According to Moya Luckett, "despite epitomizing patriarchy at its most oppressive, female-oriented television programs like *Big Love* [scripted drama about a polygamist family, 2006–11], *The Girls Next Door* [docusoap following Hugh Hefner and his girlfriends at the Playboy mansion, 2005–10], and *Sister Wives* . . . have reclaimed polygamy for women" (2014, 1). Luckett argues that these shows reframe a patriarchal, traditionally oppressive lifestyle as an arena of "female friendship, domestic help, and self-actualization" for women. By creating ties between women, regardless of the man of the house, the women of *Sister Wives*, who have noted several times that they intend to remain together even if their husband dies, reflect women's ties in a patriarchal society, both connecting to each other and to other series of women's sisterhood in patriarchal circumstances, thus expressing resistance to the centralization of men.

This intertextual sisterhood is repeated in *Girls, Desperate Housewives, The Real Housewives*, and to a certain extent, in *Grey's Anatomy* and *Six Feet Under* as well, despite that the latter two series include men characters in their ensembles. The 2010 *Girls* premiere exemplifies a women's television intertextuality as it directly references both *Sex and the City* and *The Mary Tyler Moore Show*, immediately positioning *Girls* amid women-led televisual texts. *Girls* thus sets the tone of its thematic foci regarding issues of women's work, friendship, sexuality, family, and more via intertextuality with both the 1970s second-wave workplace sitcom and the 2000s third-wave sex dramedy.[21]

On a similar note, *Insecure*'s (2016–) pilot explicitly references *Girlfriends* (2000–2008), which places it in the realm of women's shows revolving around sex, dating, work, and friendship and also in line with shows that focus on Black women, honing in on the sex, dating, work, and friendships of Black women. Similarly, *The Real Housewives* docusoap franchise's debut in 2006 with *The Real Housewives of Orange County* set out to present the reality version of *Desperate Housewives* (2004–12). The president of the Bravo broadcasting network at the time stated in a press release announcing the airing of the show, "here is a series that depicts real-life 'desperate' housewives with an authentic look at their compelling day-to-day drama" (Zalaznick, quoted in Rogers 2006). Many twenty-first-century chick TV series initially position themselves in intertextuality with women's culture, as if working together to rewrite narrative tradition.

Correspondingly, the pilot episode of *Nurse Jackie* opens in a white room with Jackie lying on the floor in a mid-twentieth-century nurse uniform. Though the rest of the episode is set in a twenty-first-century present, the first image establishes an intertextual mode, by which Jackie echoes the characterization of nurses of early television representations with the likes of nurse Liz Thorpe of *The Nurses* (1962–65) and nurse Julia Baker of *Julia* (1968–71), both kindhearted and maternal as well as dependable and professional nurses. The stylistic reference in *Nurse Jackie* connects the nurses to each other and creates a web of feminine performances that deal with care, work, and family. Moreover, the first scene foreshadows the reverie sequence in the season finale (season 1, episode 12, "Health Care & Cinema"), with Jackie dressed in the retro nurse uniform, this time also envisioning her family members dressed in midcentury garb, waving in front

---

21. In the third season's seventh episode, *Girls* also directly references Jane Austen, positioning itself as part of a tradition of women's culture.

of a suburban house. Thus, Jackie intertextualizes not only with working women but also with domestic women in the history of televisual representation.

Unlike her predecessors, however, Jackie's representational context allows for explicit antiheroinism, such that involves sexuality and substance abuse, thereby pushing back against social constructions regarding women's propriety. By positioning Jackie vis-à-vis her precursors, her character both repeats women's representation and transforms it—in effect, her character is antiheroinized. Furthermore, Jackie's transformative antiheroinism sheds new light on the more subtle resistances of the women characters in television representations prior to the twenty-first century.

Other than intertextual references to older televisual "sisters," twenty-first-century chick TV series repeat intertextual ties across contemporaneous texts. For that matter, Jackie's characterization as an adulterous wife poses her in comparison with past characters, such as *Peyton Place*'s (1964–69) Julie Anderson or *Dynasty*'s (1981–89) Alexis Carrington, and also with contemporaneous characters, such as *Desperate Housewives*' Gabrielle Solis and *How to Get Away with Murder*'s Annalise Keating, all of whom cheated on their husbands under various circumstances. Similarly, Jackie's characterization as an addict situates her among other televisual women addicts, from *Dallas*'s (1978–91) Sue Ellen Ewing and her struggles with alcohol to the more recent *Orange Is the New Black*'s (2013–19) Nicky Nichols and her struggles with drugs. When read intertextually—against the backdrop of women's drinking as a symptom of depression resulting from abuse and oppression or infidelity as a form of acting out against manipulation and corruption—Jackie's antiheroinism, though reflecting choices that are themselves manipulative or even abusive to others, reveals as much about social and gender constructs as about her specific story.[22]

---

22. Susan Faludi notes that "the women who go mad in the 1970s women's films are . . . suburban housewives driven batty by subordination, repression, drudgery, and neglect. . . . In *Diary of a Mad Housewife* . . . and *A Woman Under the*

Of course, chick TV intertextuality runs through various texts, not only non-TV women's culture but also TV that is non-chick. *Nurse Jackie* is a prominent example as its star Edie Falco inevitably intertextualizes with her iconic role as *The Sopranos*' Carmela, whom she played right before assuming the role of Jackie Peyton. Furthermore, *Nurse Jackie*'s pilot intertextualizes with the pilot episode of another arguably pointedly "masculine" text, *Mad Men*. Both *Nurse Jackie* and *Mad Men* follow a day in the professional and sexual lives of their respective protagonists until revealing, during the very final minutes of each episode, that each protagonist is married with children (McNutt 2009). *Nurse Jackie* obviously also intertextualizes with hospital shows that focus on men characters or ensemble casts (such as *House*, *St. Elsewhere*, or *ER*), as *Six Feet Under* intertextualizes with non-chick family dramas (*Here and Now*, *Parenthood*) and *The Real Housewives* franchise intertextualizes with non-chick docusoaps (such as *Shahs of Sunset* or *Jersey Shore*). Nevertheless, though intertextuality of chick TV antiheroines with non-chick TV antiheroes or texts may offer resistance to normative structures, it is the ties between chick TV antiheroines that accumulate resistances to said structures from the margins.

Reading the web of televisual antiheroines intertextually perceives these women as a group conducting "relationships with other women outside of their familial roles as wives and mothers" and envisioning "alternative lifestyles for women based upon meaningful social relationships with other women" (Ball 2013, 246), not only within their worlds but also intertextually. Through intertextual repetition, antiheroines reiterate the actions of one another and influence each other; their resistances gather to reread and rewrite narrative and social order, effecting repetition as transgression (Deleuze 1994), intertextuality as transformation (Kristeva 1980). Thus, the antiheroine-televisual web,

---

Influence . . . , the wives' pill-popping habits and nervous breakdowns are presented as not-so-unreasonable responses to their crippling domestic condition—madness as a sign of their underlying sanity. What the male characters label lunacy in these films usually turns out to be a form of feminist resistance" (1991, 124).

constructed of the various representations of antiheroines, functions as an ontological bridge through which characters and themes interlace and feed each other. This cross-referential, transgressive, and transformative web of chick TV antiheroines creates an alternative order, one in which women's identity is not determined in accordance with that of men but rather in relation to other women in the chick TV sphere.

Conclusion

Reclaiming "Chick" for TV

This book has examined forms of textual resistance in twenty-first-century chick TV, focusing on the ties between temporal and characterizational resistances. The chapters were dedicated to layers of temporal-antiheroinist challenges to chrononormative order—implicit antiheroinism in the intradiegesis, explicit antiheroinism inscribed in the text via temporal constructs, serialized antiheroinism through the structure of seriality, and a transformative antiheroinism rewritten and rewriting via intertextual repetition. Chapter 1, "Resistance," revealed the feminist politics at the foundation of chick TV and stressed that the insistence of chick TV texts to tell women's stories is a form of feminist resistance to the traditional marginalization and devaluation of women's culture. The chapter analyzed several intradiegetic narrative devices that work to delay the narrative temporal flow, thereby resisting chrononormativity, as seen in *Girls*' story-within-story, *Nurse Jackie*'s reverie, *Six Feet Under*'s fantasy sequences, *Being Mary Jane*'s "live" segments, and *The Real Housewives*' confessionals—subatomic (perhaps subepisodic) resistances in the chick TV text.

While chapter 1 demonstrated that chick TV is at its core a resistant subgenre by examining implicit temporal resistances in the texts, chapter 2, "Deviation," turned to explicit narrative resistances as manifested in temporal deviations—flashback, flashforward, flash-sideways. Though not unique to chick TV, when these flashes are featured in chick TV texts, they become political tools of feminist resistance as they deviate from order, as can be seen in the main case study of the chapter,

Grey's Anatomy, and the comparative analyses of *Six Feet Under* and *Desperate Housewives*. By reexamining women's choices regarding performances of femininity, the temporal flashes offer resistance to social scripts and allow renegotiation of the social, gendered order.

This resistance is further complicated as discussed in chapter 3, "Serialization," which demonstrated that chick TV texts, even if they do not promote feminist resistance in the plotline, may do so in the structure of their serial form, interpreted via intratextual, comparative analysis of units within the series (episodes/seasons). Seriality is thus a form of temporal resistance that can either reinforce the diegetic or narrative resistance each episode presents or generate a textual temporal resistance for ostensibly nonresistant episodes. This paradigm was exemplified via analyses of the ties between seasons and episodes by focusing on the seriality of *The Real Housewives* franchise, in which "real housewives" seem to adhere to hegemonic order in the plot but under serialized reading undergo antiheroinization. Here, any antiheroinist resistances suppressed in the creases of the chick TV text are revealed when the text is spread out and reread serially rather than episodically.

Finally, chapter 4, "Rewriting," looked at the intertextual web that can be drawn between various chick TV texts and their resistant antiheroines in an attempt to identify an intertextual form of resistance, a resistance that is manifested in the repetitions between the texts. Analyzing "excesses" along the sexual and domestic continua, the discussion focused on *Desperate Housewives* and the intertextual repetitions it draws and argued that twenty-first-century chick TV functions in cross-referential reflexivity, referencing both the tradition of women's culture and contemporaneous chick TV texts. Whether each text is resistant or not, the cumulative value of performances of femininity exposes the arbitrariness of gendered culture and consequently contests the marginalization of chick TV. The intertextual ties between resistant women antiheroinizes them in creating a transformative form of repetition that rewrites narrative order and offers new strategies for the characterization of antiheroines.

Each temporal layer of chick TV—intradiegetic, episodic, serial, and intertextual—exhibits some degree of temporal-antiheroinist resistance, whether explicitly or through textual analysis. It bears inquiring, however—is every form of resistance the same as the other? If both intradiegetic and serial resistances are revealed through textual reading, how do they differ? If both serial and intertextual resistances are brought about via examination of the ties between textual units, do they generate different forms of resistance? I contend that each level of resistance bears a certain idiosyncrasy, as each layer of temporality not only conducts a different interrelation with antiheroinism but also reflects a different form of antiheroinism.

When antiheroinism is manifested in the intradiegetic temporal level, it presents itself as a *culturally resistant antiheroinism*, which defies patriarchal culture by favoring women's culture. Antiheroinism that is detected in the episodic level (via flashes) is presented as a *socially resistant antiheroinism* that challenges patriarchal order by opting out of patriarchal demands to "maintain, arrange, and perpetuate this sociosymbolic contract as mothers, wives, nurses, doctors, teachers" (Kristeva 1981, 23–24). "Serial" antiheroinism is not necessarily imprinted in the text but, rather, stems from serialization, from the comparison between performances of femininity in the series. It is thus a *textually resistant antiheroinism*, enhancing singular episodic resistances or antiheroinizing conservative performances of femininity. Finally, reading the repetitions of the intertextual web of chick TV antiheroines reveals a *televisually resistant antiheroinism*, the defiance of which emerges from the accumulation of representations of antiheroinism that are reflexively aware of other televisual representations, including those to which they resist. Intertextual antiheroinism is thus transformative antiheroinism, as it is based on the amassing resistances of antiheroines of all types across chick TV texts and effectively offers an alternative televisual order based on women's culture rather than on traditional (patriarchal) narrative and social order.

Of course, antiheroinism can appear in more than one temporal layer of each text. Arguably, it appears in the intertextual layer in all

Table 2
Chick TV Temporality and Antiheroinism

Link between temporality and antiheroinism	Layer of temporality	Temporal resistance	Degree of antiheroinism	Form of antiheroinism	Relationship to hegemonic order
Resistance	Intra-diegetic temporality—Sub-textual Sub-episodic Intra-diegetic	*Delay* of hegemonic time and order—subtextually insisting on "feminine" culture	Implied in the text—antiheroinism revealed through textual analysis	Cultural antiheroinism. Resisting patriarchal order by favoring women's culture	*Resisting* hegemonic order by envisioning an alternative order
Deviation	*Episodic temporality*—Textual Episodic Diegetic	*Deviation* from the time of history—a separate temporal realm (flashes) offered textually (rather than subtextually)	Explicit in the text—antiheroinism written into the plot, explicated via temporal analysis	Social antiheroinism. One challenging patriarchal order by opting out of patriarchal demands towards women—to nurture, to mother, to nest	*Deviating* from hegemonic order to practice alternative order (though antiheroine changes, hegemonic order continues after deviation)
Serialization	*Serial temporality*—Intra-textual Serial Extra-diegetic	*Serialization* of forms of antiheroinism—bending the time of history into serialized (or matrixialized) performances and mis-performances of femininity	Implied in the text—the episodes may perpetuate hegemonic order or represent singular resistances, but serial analysis exposes antiheroinism by creating comparisons that clarify gender's constructedness	Serial/serialized antiheroinism. challenging patriarchal order via comparison between serial/serialized performances of femininity, emphasizing gender performances' constructedness	*Serializing* disruptions to the hegemonic order, thereby exposing its arbitrariness and constructedness
Intertextuality	*Intertextual temporality*—Extra-textual Repetitious Rhizomatic Meta-diegetic	*Repetition* of forms of antiheroinism—rewriting the time of history with a system of accumulating resisting repetitions	Either implied or explicit— Intertextual reading of antiheroinist repetitions bolsters antiheroinism	Intertextual/chick-TV antiheroinism. challenging patriarchal order via repetition and accumulation of representations. Various forms of antiheroinism join to rewrite order	*Rewriting* an alternative order, by intertextualizing multiple antiheroinisms—hegemonic order is not only delayed, but sidestepped

chick TV and most likely in at least one more layer, depending on the text's feminist politics. Table 2 delineates the layers of temporality and antiheroinism and their ties to order.

Eventually, the network of chronoresistant, antiheroinist chick TV creates its own narrative order, a sisterhood of antiheroines formed by intertextual bonds and built not in relation to or in juxtaposition with men's culture but in continuity of the lineage of women's culture—the woman's novel, the woman's film, chick-lit and chick flicks, melodramas and soap operas, all of which were traditionally marginalized but later academically reclaimed.

Textual subversions of hegemonic practice are relevant not only in terms of feminist resistance but also in terms of other marginalized cultures, such as textual racial resistance and textual queer resistance. Emma LaRocque, for example, notes that artistic resistance of a suppressed racial group must be expressed in the humanization of its characters such that the characters' humanity does not "have to part the seas of abstract collectivities, be they negative or romanticized, trip over anthropologists or typologies," before it can be appreciated (2010, 158). Thus, LaRocque distinguishes between resisting dehumanization and restoring humanity. Correspondingly, Frederik Dhaenens and Sofie Van Bauwel distinguish between deconstructive queer resistance, which "points out how gender and sexual identities are presumed to be "fixed" by discursive practices" (2012, 712), and reconstructive queer resistance, which involves "the rearticulation of gender and sexual identities" and focuses on "the embodiment of gender and sexual identities that are defying and transgressing the heteronormal" (712). These models apply to feminist resistance that arises from the correlation between temporal play and antiheroinism. The tension between chick TV's antiheroinist delay of or departure from hegemonic order (as in chapters 1, 2, and 3) and the antiheroinist vision or creation of an alternative order (as in chapter 4) can be read as the tension between deconstructive and reconstructive resistance, between resisting dehumanization and restoring humanity.

Of course, queer and racial resistances can be amalgamated with feminist resistance on chick TV, as in the case of women of color, such as *Grey's Anatomy*'s Asian American Cristina Yang and African American Miranda Bailey, *Being Mary Jane*'s African American Mary Jane Paul, and *Desperate Housewives*' Latina Gabrielle Solis, and LBT women, such as *Grey's Anatomy*'s bisexual Callie Torres, *Transparent*'s transgender woman Maura, bisexual Sarah, and lesbian Ali Pfefferman, and *Desperate Housewives*' bisexual Katherine Mayfair. These intersectional antiheroines struggle not only with gender expectations but also with racial and/or sexual expectations, thereby exposing other social mechanisms beyond gender-based ones.

As these comparisons to other forms of textual resistance suggest, that an art form is marginalized does not strip it of its political, transformative power. Indeed, quite the contrary. This book joins the feminist project that has been toiling "to render visible the invisible (and often culturally disregarded)" (Brunsdon, D'Acci, Spigel 1997, 6)—insisting that women's culture, indeed "often culturally disregarded" as superficial pulp, comprises rich, complex, and political art forms. Feminist endeavors to reclaim the artistic value of women's culture were manifested in research (Modleski 2007 [1982]), on the woman's novel (Showalter 1977; Beer, 1974), the woman's film (Kaplan 1983; Modleski 2002), chick-lit (Gill and Herdieckerhoff 2006; Ferriss and Young 2006), chick flicks (Rich 1998; Ferriss and Young 2008), and soap operas (Lopate 1977; Modleski 1979). In turn, this book insists on reclaiming "chick" for TV, insisting that "girly," "soapy," "trash," "chick" TV, often dismissed as inferior, in fact possesses textual, narrative, temporal, and characterizational complexities and, when read closely in search of its complexities, is, contrary to common criticism, political, resistant, and radical.

As such, the television antiheroine has not been truly absent, as suggested by twenty-first-century scholars and critics (Poniewozik and Winters 2007; Mittell 2015a); she has simply been "hiding" in the temporal creases of the often-snubbed world of chick TV rather than residing in other, more acclaimed, more covered, and more researched genres. For twenty-first-century US TV antiheroines, the radical feminist project is not about inclusion in "the antihero clubhouse" (Menon 2008). It is about acknowledging that antiheroines have long had an established club, an arguably underground club, but one definitely complex and sophisticated in its own right that upholds women's culture while also transforming it—chick TV.

Appendix

References

Index

Appendix

Antiheroines Positioned along the Continua

According to the model I charted, by which antiheroinism is examined along four continua—the domestic continuum, the sexual continuum, the intellectual continuum, and the class continuum—a heroine would be a woman character who fairs evenly on each of the continua; she would be domestic but not "obsessively" so, attractive but not "too sexual," clever but not opinionated, elegant but not snobbish. Comparatively conservative televisual representation could fall into that category, such as Harriet Nelson of *The Adventures of Ozzie and Harriet* (1952–66), Margaret Anderson of *Father Knows Best* (1954–60), or June Cleaver of *Leave It to Beaver* (1957–63). Of course, there are later representations of "perfect" TV heroines, but these early television representations in many ways set the stage for the characterization of "good" women on American television.

Conversely, the antiheroines of chick TV stray from the continua's medians, thereby defining their antiheroinism, either positioned too high or too low along these continua. The following list maps out the antiheroines analyzed in the book according to their positions on each of the continua. The list is a somewhat reductive classification of complex antiheroinist characters for the sake of positioning the case studies within the analytical framework. It must not be read as the author's personal judgment but rather as an attempt to reflect the social judgment that would be cast upon these women under a patriarchal order and sometimes is indeed cast—by other characters in the text, by the text itself in tone or mise-en-scène, or by extratextual viewers and critics—as demonstrated throughout this book. It is these judged categories that *Chick TV: Antiheroines and Time Unbound* has set out to reconsider as antiheroinist resistance to the policing of feminine performance.

Christine Brown. One of the main cast members of *Sister Wives*, Christine is perceived as "not sexual enough," covertly comparing herself to her husband's more desired wife, and as "too domestic," caring for the household at the expense of other things. Consequently, she is perceived as too simple or unsophisticated and as insufficiently elegant.

Janelle Brown. One of the main cast members of *Sister Wives*, Janelle is perceived as "not sexual enough" (this is implied, but never spoken) and as "not domestic enough," as she prefers work life to homemaking. She is perceived as too sophisticated and as insufficiently elegant.

Cynthia Bailey. One of the cast members of *The Real Housewives of Atlanta*, Cynthia is perceived as too vain regarding her sexual attractiveness; as "not domestic enough" as wife and mother; as too vociferous; and as snobbish by some while "low-class" by others.

Miranda Bailey. One of the main characters of *Grey's Anatomy*, Miranda starts out as "not too sexual," as her sexuality is not addressed, but becomes sexual with her second husband later in the series; perceived as "not domestic enough" in the eyes of her first husband early in the series and "too domestic" in the eyes of her coworkers after giving birth to her first child (perceived as having become too "soft"). She is perceived as sharp and bossy, referred to as "the Nazi," and as indifferent to class.

Brenda Chenowith. One of the main characters of *Six Feet Under*, Brenda is perceived as "too sexual," as she has multiple sexual partners, including while in committed relationships. She starts out as "not domestic enough" in her desire to escape domesticity but becomes "too domestic" and perceived as too insistent on family life. She is highly intelligent, to the point that she is seen as argumentative, and she resists her parents' upper-class pedigree.

Claire Fisher. One of the main characters of *Six Feet Under*, Claire could be perceived as "too sexual" for experimenting with multiple partners and not for reproductive purposes; as "not domestic enough," as she does not want to care for others or the household. She is seen as an independent thinker, by some as too independent, and as someone who does not follow decorum.

Ruth Fisher. One of *Six Feet Under*'s main characters, Ruth starts out as "not sexual enough" and is later perceived as "too sexual" (for her age); as "too domestic" and entrenched in housewifery to the point of sacrificing other pursuits; as "simple"; and as clueless in terms of Los Angeles class culture.

Teresa Giudice. One of the cast members of *The Real Housewives of New Jersey*, Teresa is perceived as "too sexual"—though she practices sexuality only with her husband, her "excessive" sexuality is often addressed; as "too domestic," depicted as obsessed with caring for the home at the expense of other things; as "dumb"; and as "class-less."

Meredith Grey. The protagonist of *Grey's Anatomy*, Meredith fluctuates between extremes, as she starts out as "too sexual" for sleeping with various partners, including a married man, and as reluctant to commit to relationships but then becomes monogamous and later "not sexual enough" and reluctant to enter into new relationships after her husband dies. She starts out as "not domestic enough" but becomes "too domestic" as she puts home and children before everything else. She is perceived as driven and opinionated and as disinterested in etiquette codes, though she is obviously of the middle class.

Hannah Horvath. The protagonist of *Girls*, Hannah is perceived as "too sexual" as she experiments with her sexuality; as "not domestic enough" since she is not family-oriented (though enters motherhood in the series finale); as a wiseacre; and as vulgar.

Kenya Moore. One of the cast members of *The Real Housewives of Atlanta*, Kenya is perceived as "too sexual" and portrayed as immodest in her sexuality; as both "not domestic enough" and "too domestic," as she lacks domestic skills but seems to pursue domesticity too enthusiastically; as condescending; and both as a snob and as uncouth.

Mary Jane Paul. The protagonist of *Being Mary Jane*, Mary Jane is perceived as "too sexual" because she sleeps with a married man and has multiple partners; as "too domestic" since she is eager to assume domestic roles and often perceived as too enthusiastic about entering into marriage and motherhood;

as too complicated and career-oriented; and as snobbish, adopting upper-class traits of which her working-class family is critical.

Jackie Peyton. The protagonist of *Nurse Jackie*, Jackie is perceived as "too sexual" as she is unfaithful to her husband; as "not domestic enough," as she is framed as under-caring for her home and children; as opinionated; and as resisting ladylike behavior.

Gabrielle Solis. One of the main characters of *Desperate Housewives*, Gabrielle is perceived as "too sexual" because she cheats on her husband; as "not domestic enough" since she has an aversion to all things domestic and familial; as opinionated; and as pretentious.

Bree van de Kamp. One of *Desperate Housewives*' main characters, Bree starts out as "not sexual enough" and later is perceived as "too sexual" when she engages in depression-induced sexual pursuits; she is perceived as "too domestic"; often criticized for being too opinionated; and seen as a snob and too mindful of issues of etiquette.

Cristina Yang. One of *Grey's Anatomy*'s main characters, Cristina is perceived as "too sexual" as she is interested in sex but not emotions, at least in the first seasons; as "not domestic enough" because she does not want to have children and stays away from all things domestic (does not cook or clean); as bright and conceited; and as disinterested in class (though inadequate in comparison to her fiancé's family in early seasons).

References

Adams, Percy G. 1976. "The Anti-Hero in Eighteenth-Century Fiction." *Studies in the Literary Imagination* 9, no. 1 (Spring): 29–51.

Akass, Kim. 2005. "Mother Knows Best: Ruth and Representations of Mothering in *Six Feet Under*." In *Reading "Six Feet Under": TV to Die For*, edited by Kim Akass and Janet McCabe, 110–20. London: I. B. Tauris.

Akass, Kim, and Janet McCabe. 2005. *Reading "Six Feet Under": TV to Die For*. London: I. B. Tauris.

Allan, Alexandra Jane. 2009. "The Importance of Being a 'Lady': Hyper-Femininity and Heterosexuality in the Private, Single-Sex Primary School." *Gender and Education* 21 (2): 145–58.

Allen, Robert C. 1985. *Speaking of Soap Operas*. Chapel Hill: Univ. of North Carolina Press.

Alsop, Elizabeth. 2019. "Sorority Flow: The Rhetoric of Sisterhood in Post-Network Television." *Feminist Media Studies* 19 (7): 1026–42.

Ames, Melissa, ed. 2012. *Time in Television Narrative: Exploring Temporality in Twenty-First-Century Programming*. Jackson: Univ. Press of Mississippi.

Attwood, Feona. 2007. "Sluts and Riot Grrrls: Female Identity and Sexual Agency." *Journal of Gender Studies* 16 (3): 233–47.

Ball, Vicky. 2013. "Forgotten Sisters: The British Female Ensemble Drama." *Screen* 54 (2): 244–48.

Barker, David. 1988. "It's Been Real: Forms of Television Representation." *Critical Studies in Mass Communication* 5: 42–56.

Barthes, Roland. 1977. *Image, Music, Text*. Translated by Stephen Heath. New York: Hill and Wang.

Beer, Patricia. 1974. *Reader, I married him: A Study of the Women Characters of Jane Austen, Charlotte Brontë, Elizabeth Gaskell and George Eliot*. New York: Springer.

Bennet, Lucy. 2012. "Lost in Time?: *Lost* Fan Engagement with Temporal Play." In *Time in Television Narrative: Exploring Temporality in Twenty-First-Century Programming*, edited by Melissa Ames, 279–309. Jackson: Univ. Press of Mississippi.

Biederer, Barbara. 2016. "'Do You Know' of the Conflict of Having a Family and Career as a Female Surgeon? The Representation of Cristina Yang in ABC's *Grey's Anatomy*." *Current Objectives of Postgraduate American Studies* 17 (2): 1–10.

Blumenthal, Dannielle. 1997. *Women and Soap Opera: A Cultural Feminist Perspective*. Westport, CT: Praeger Publishers.

Boone, Joseph Allen. 1987. *Tradition Counter Tradition: Love and the Form of Fiction*. Chicago: Univ. of Chicago Press.

Booth, Paul. 2011. "Memories, Temporalities, Fictions: Temporal Displacement in Contemporary Television." *Television & New Media* 12(4): 370–88.

———. 2012. *Time on TV: Temporal Displacement and Mashup Television*. New York: Peter Lang.

Bourdieu, Pierre. 1984. *Distinction: A Social Critique of the Judgment of Taste*. Translated by Richard Nice. Cambridge, MA: Harvard Univ. Press.

Bradshaw, Lara. 2013. "Showtime's 'Female Problem': Cancer, Quality and Motherhood." *Journal of Consumer Culture* 13 no. 2 (July): 160–77.

Brand, Madeleine. 2009. "Bravo Exec on the Art of Creating 'Reality.'" *All Things Considered*. National Public Radio, August 12, 2009.

Brombert, Victor. 1999. *In Praise of Antiheroes: Figures and Themes in Modern European Literature 1830–1980*. Chicago: Univ. of Chicago Press.

Brooks Higginbotham, Evelyn. 1993. *Righteous Discontent: The Women's Movement in the Black Baptist Church, 1880–1920*. Cambridge, MA: Harvard Univ. Press.

Brost, Molly J. 2020. *The Anti-Heroine on Contemporary Television: Transgressive Women*. Lanham, MD: Lexington Books.

Brunsdon, Charlotte. 1995. "The Role of Soap Opera in the Development of Feminist Television Scholarship." In *To be Continued . . . : Soap Operas Around the World*, edited by Robert Clyde Allen, 49–65. London: Routledge.

———. 2000. *The Feminist, the Housewife, and the Soap Opera*. Oxford: Oxford Univ. Press.

Brunsdon, Charlotte, Julie D'Acci, and Lynn Spiegel. 1997. "Introduction." In *Feminist Television Criticism: A Reader*, edited by Charlotte Brunsdon, Julie D'Acci, and Lynn Spiegel, 1–7. Oxford: Clarendon Press.

Bruun Vaage, Margrethe. 2016. *The Antihero in American Television*. London: Routledge.

Bryson, Valerie. 2007. *Gender and the Politics of Time: Feminist Theory and Contemporary Debates*. Bristol: Policy Press.

Buonanno, Milly, ed. 2017. *Television Antiheroines: Women Behaving Badly in Crime and Prison Drama*. Chicago: Univ. of Chicago Press and The Mill.

Burkhead, Cynthia, and Hillary Robson, eds. 2008. *Grace Under Pressure: Grey's Anatomy Uncovered*. Newcastle, UK: Cambridge Scholars Publishing.

Burns-Ardolino, Wendy A. 2016. *TV Female Foursomes and Their Fans: Featuring "The Golden Girls," "Designing Women," "Living Single," "Sex and the City," "Girlfriends," "Cashmere Mafia," and "Hot in Cleveland."* Jefferson, NC: McFarland & Co.

Butler, Jeremy. 1993. "Redesigning Discourse: Feminism, the Sitcom, and *Designing Women*." *Journal of Film and Video* 45 (1): 13–26.

Butler, Judith. 1988. "Performative Acts and Gender Constitution." *Theatre Journal* 40, no. 4 (December): 519–31.

———. 1990. "Gender Trouble." In *Feminism/Postmodernism*, edited by Linda J. Nicholson, 324–40. New York: Routledge.

Byars, Jackie. 1991. *All That Hollywood Allows: Re-reading Gender in 1950s Melodrama*. London: Routledge.

Cain, James Mallahan. 1941. *Mildred Pierce*. New York: Alfred A. Knopf.

Cartridge, Neil, ed. 2012. *Heroes and Anti-heroes in Medieval Romance*. Cambridge: Boydell & Brewer.

Cassillo, John. 2018. "Which Real Housewives Audiences Overlap Most Within the Franchise?" *Nexttv.com*. August 24, 2018. https://www.nexttv.com/news/which-real-housewives-audiences-overlap-most-within-franchise.

Cheah, Pheng, Elizabeth Grosz, Judith Butler, and Drucilla Cornell. 1998. "The Future of Sexual Difference: An Interview with Judith Butler and Drucilla Cornell," *Diacritics* 28, no. 1 (Irigaray and the Political Future of Sexual Difference, Spring): 19–42.

Chen, Fanfan. 2008. "From Hypotyposis to Metalepsis: Narrative Devices in Contemporary Fantastic Fiction." *Forum for Modern Language Studies* 44, no. 4 (October): 394–411.

Christian, Aymar Jean. 2010. "On Cable, Long Live the Anti-Hero." *Televisual.org*, March 29, 2010. http://tvisual.org/2010/03/29/on-cable-long-live-the-anti-hero/.

Cixous, Hélèn. 1981. "Castration or Decapitation?" Translated by Annette Kuhn. *Signs* 7, no. 1 (Autumn): 36–40.

Clarke, M. J. 2013. "*Lost* and Mastermind Narration." In *Transmedia Television: New Trends in Network Serial Production*, 123–42. New York: Bloomsbury.

Clavel-Vazquez, Adriana. 2018. "Sugar and Spice, and Everything Nice: What Rough Heroines Tell Us about Imaginative Resistance." *The Journal of Aesthetics and Art Criticism* 76, no. 2 (Spring): 202–12.

Connell, R. W. 1995. *Masculinities*. Berkeley: Univ. of California Press.

Coward, Rosalind. 2006. "Still Desperate: Popular Television and the Female Zeitgeist." In *Reading "Desperate Housewives": Beyond the White Picket Fence*, edited by Janet McCabe and Kim Akass, 31–41. London: I. B. Tauris.

Cox, Nicole B., and Jennifer M. Proffitt. 2012. "The Housewives' Guide to Better Living: Promoting Consumption on Bravo's *The Real Housewives*." *Communication, Culture & Critique* 5, no. 2 (June): 295–312.

Creeber, Glen. 2004. *Serial Television: Big Drama on the Small Screen*. London: BFI Publishing.

D'Acci, Julie. 1994. *Defining Women: Television and the Case of Cagney & Lacey*. Chapel Hill: Univ. of North Carolina Press.

Deleuze, Gilles. 1989. *Cinema II: The Time Image*. Minneapolis: Univ. of Minnesota Press. First published 1985.

———. 1994. *Difference and Repetition*. New York: Columbia Univ. Press. First published in 1968.

Deleuze, Gilles, and Félix Guattari. 1986. *Kafka: Toward a Minor Literature*, translated by Dana Polan. Theory and History of Literature Series. Minneapolis: Univ. of Minnesota Press.

———. 2003. "Introduction." In *A Thousand Plateaus: Capitalism and Schizophrenia*, translated by Brian Massumi, 3–28. London: Continuum. First published in 1980.

Dhaenens, Frederik, and Sofie Van Bauwel. 2012. "The Good, the Bad or the Queer: Articulations of Queer Resistance in *The Wire*." *Sexualities* 15 (5/6): 702–17.

Doane, Mary Ann. 1982. "Film and the Masquerade: Theorizing the Female Spectator." *Screen* 23 (3–4): 74–87.

Dominguez, Pier. 2015. "'I'm Very Rich, Bitch!': The Melodramatic Money Shot and the Excess of Racialized Gendered Affect in the *Real Housewives* Docusoaps." *Camera Obscura* 30, no. 1 (88): 155–83.

Dunham, Lena. 2014. *Not That Kind of Girl*. New York: Random House.

Eco, Umberto. 1985. "Innovation and Repetition: Between Modern and Postmodern Aesthetics." *Daedalus* 114, no. 4 (Fall): 191–207.

Edgerton, Gary. 2007. *The Columbia History of American Television*. New York: Columbia Univ. Press.

Elliott, Jane. 2008. "Stepford U.S.A.: Second-Wave Feminism, Domestic Labor, and the Representation of National Time." *Cultural Critique* 70 (Fall): 32–62.

Ellis, John. 2000. *Seeing Things: Television in the Age of Uncertainty*. London: I. B. Tauris.

Ettinger, Bracha. 1995. *The Matrixial Gaze*. Leeds: Univ. of Leeds.

———. 2001. "Wit(h)nessing Trauma and the Matrixial Gaze: From Phantasm to Trauma, from Phallic Structure to Matrixial Sphere." *Parallax* 7 (4): 89–114.

Faludi, Susan. 1991. *Backlash: The Undeclared War against American Women*. New York: Doubleday.

Ferriss, Suzanne, and Mallory Young, eds. 2006. *Chick Lit: The New Woman's Fiction*. New York: Routledge.

———, eds. 2008. *Chick Flicks: Contemporary Women at the Movies*. New York: Routledge.

Feuer, Jane. 1983. "The Concept of Live Television: Ontology as Ideology." In *Regarding Television: Critical Approaches—An Anthology*, edited by E. A. Kaplan, 12–21. Los Angeles: American Film Institute.

Fiske, John. 1987. *Television Culture*. London: Routledge.

Freeman, Elizabeth. 2010. *Time Binds: Queer Temporalities, Queer Histories*. Durham, NC: Duke Univ. Press.

Friedan, Betty. 1970. *The Feminine Mystique*. New York: Dell. First published 1963.

Fuchs, Michael. 2012. "'Play It Again, Sam . . . and Dean': Temporality and Meta-Textuality in *Supernatural*." In *Time in Television Narrative: Exploring Temporality in Twenty-First-Century Programming*, edited by Melissa Ames, 82–94. Jackson: Univ. Press of Mississippi.

Gamson, Joshua. 1998. *Freaks Talk Back: Tabloid Talk Shows and Sexual Nonconformity*. Chicago: Univ. of Chicago Press.

Ganguly, Keya. 2004. "Temporality and Postcolonial Critique." In *The Cambridge Companion to Postcolonial Literary Studies*, edited by Neil Lazarus, 162–81. Cambridge: Cambridge Univ. Press.

Garbarz, Franck F. 2013. *The Emergence of the Anti-hero in American Cinema from the 1960s to the 1990s*. Course description for Institut d'Etudes Politiques de Paris. Spring semester. http://formation.sciences-po.fr/enseignement/2013/dhum/1190a.

Genette, Gérard. 1980. *Narrative Discourse*. Translated by Jane E. Lewin. Ithaca, NY: Cornell Univ. Press. First published 1972.

Gill, Rosalind, and Elena Herdieckerhoff. 2006. "Rewriting the Romance: New Femininities in Chick Lit?" *Feminist Media Studies* 6 (4): 487–504.

Gilman, Sander L. 1985. "Black Bodies, White Bodies: Toward an Iconography of Female Sexuality in Late Nineteenth Century Art, Medicine, and Literature." *Critical Inquiry* 12 (1): 204–42.

Gray, James J., and Rebecca L. Ginsberg. 2007. "Muscle Dissatisfaction: An Overview of Psychological and Cultural Research and Theory." In *The Muscular Ideal: Psychological, Social, and Medical Perspectives*, edited by J. Kevin Thompson and Guy Cafri, 15–39. Washington, DC: American Psychological Association.

Grdešić, Maša. 2013. "'I'm Not the Ladies!': Metatextual Commentary in *Girls*." *Feminist Media Studies* 13 (2): 355–58.

Griffiths, Jay. 1999. *Pip Pip: A Sideways Look at Time*. London: Flamingo.

Haas, Melanie, N. A. Pierce, and Gretchen Busl. 2020. *Antiheroines of Contemporary Media: Saints, Sinners, and Survivors*. Lanham, MD: Lexington Books.

Halberstam, J. 2005. *In a Queer Time and Place: Transgender Bodies, Subcultural Lives*. New York: New York Univ. Press.

———. 2011. *The Queer Art of Failure*. Durham, NC: Duke Univ. Press.

Hall, Stuart. 1980. "Encoding/Decoding." In *Culture, Media, Language*, edited by Dorothy Hobson, Andrew Lowe, Paul Willis, 128–38. London: Hutchinson.

Hanson, Helen, and Catherine O'Rawe, eds. 2010. *The Femme Fatale: Images, Histories, Contexts*. Basingstoke: Palgrave Macmillan.

Harzewski, Stephanie. 2006. "Tradition and Displacement in the New Novel of Manners. In *Chick Lit: The New Woman's Fiction*, edited by Suzanne Ferriss and Mallory Young, 29–46. New York: Routledge.

Hatch, Kristen. 2002. "Selling Soap: Post-War Television Soap Opera and the American Housewife." In *Small Screens, Big Ideas: Television in the 1950s*, edited by Janet Thumin, 35–49. London: I. B. Tauris.

Havas, Julia, and Maria Sulimma. 2018. "Through the Gaps of My Fingers: Genre, Femininity, and Cringe Aesthetics in Dramedy Television." *Television and New Media* 13 (1): 1–20.

Hiatt, Brian. 2017. "Lena Dunham on Ending 'Girls,' Taylor Swift and Being Blamed for Hillary's Loss." *Rolling Stone.com*. February 15. https://www.rollingstone.com/tv/tv-features/lena-dunham-on-ending-girls-taylor-swift-and-being-blamed-for-hillarys-loss-118563/.

Hill, Annette. 2005. *Reality TV: Audiences and Popular Factual Television*. New York: Routledge.

Hill Collins, Patricia. 2005. *Black Sexual Politics: African Americans, Gender, and the New Racism*. New York: Routledge.

Himsel Burcon, Sarah. 2012. "*Lost* in Our Middle Hour: Faith, Fate, and Redemption Post 9/11." In *Time in Television Narrative: Exploring Temporality in Twenty-First-Century Programming*, edited by Melissa Ames, 125–38. Jackson: Univ. Press of Mississippi.

Hobson, Dorothy. 1982. *Crossroads: The Drama of a Soap Opera*. London: Methuen.

Hohenstein, Svenja, and Katharina Thalmann. 2019. "Difficult Women: Changing Representations of Female Characters in Contemporary Television Series." *Zeitschrift Für Anglistik Und Amerikanistik*, 67 (2): 109–29.

Houdek, Matthew, and Kendall Phillips. 2020. "Rhetoric and the Temporal Turn: Race, Gender, Temporalities." *Women's Studies in Communication*. 43 (4): 369–83.

Hughes, Sarah. 2014. "Move Over, Bridget Jones: Meet the Literary Antiheroines Who Prefer Partying to Romance." *Guardian*, February 18, 2014, 13.

Hunter, Latham. 2008. "Macho Marines and Ovarian Sisters: How *Grey's Anatomy* Negotiates the Feminine into a Masculinized Professional World." In *Grace Under Pressure: Grey's Anatomy Uncovered*, edited by Cynthia Burkhead and Hillary Robson, 84–99. Newcastle, UK: Cambridge Scholars Publishing.

Hunting, Kyra. 2012. "Women Talk: Chick Lit TV and the Dialogues of Feminism." *The Communication Review* 15 (3): 187–203.

Inness, Sherrie A. 2007. "Introduction: Who Remembers Sabrina? Intelligence, Gender, and the Media." In *Geek Chic: Smart Women in Popular Culture*, edited by Sherrie A. Inness, 1–9. New York: Palgrave Macmillan.

Jacobs, Jason. 2003. *Body Trauma: The New Hospital Dramas*. London: BFI Publishing.

Jacobs, Tom. 2018. "Reality TV Perpetuates the Stereotype of the Angry African American." *Pacific Standard Magazine*, August 2, 2018. https://psmag.com/social-justice/reality-tv-perpetuates-the-stereotype-of-the-angry-african-american.

Jennings, Rebecca. 2019. "How *The Real Housewives* Built Cable TV's Biggest Fandom." *Vox.com*. November 20, 2019. https://www.vox.com/the-goods/2019/11/20/20972992/bravocon-2019-real-housewives-bravo.

Johles Forman, Frieda, ed. 1989. *Taking Our Time: Feminist Perspectives on Temporality*. Oxford: Pergamon Press.

Johnson, Derek. 2009. "The Fictional Institutions of *Lost*: World Building, Reality and the Economic Possibilities of Narrative Divergence." In *Reading Lost: Perspectives on a Hit Show*, edited by Roberta Pearson, 27–49. London: I. B. Tauris.

———. 2011. "Devaluing and Revaluing Seriality: The Gendered Discourses of Media Franchising." *Media, Culture & Society* 33 (7): 1077–93.

———. 2018. "Spin-offs, Crossovers, and World-building 'Energies.'" In *Reading Contemporary Serial Television Universes: A Narrative Ecosystem Framework*, edited by Paola Brembilla and Ilaria A. De Pascalis, 74–92. New York: Routledge.

Johnson, Merry Lisa. 2004. "Relationship Autopsy to Romantic Utopia: The Missing Discourse of Egalitarian Marriage on HBO's *Six Feet Under*." *Discourse* 26 (3): 18–40.

Jorgenson, Derek A. 2014. "Media and Polygamy: A Critical Analysis of *Sister Wives*." *Communication Studies* 65 (1): 24–38.

Joyrich, Lynne. 2004. "Written on the Screen: Mediation and Immersion in *Far from Heaven*." *Camera Obscura* 19 (3): 186–219.

Kanazawa, Satoshi. 2011. "Why Are Black Women Less Physically Attractive Than Other Women." *The Scientific Fundamentalist Online Blog* (withdrawn).

Kaplan, E. Ann. 1983. "Theories of Melodrama: A Feminist Perspective." *Women & Performance: A Journal of Feminist Theory* 1 (1): 40–48.

Kelly, J. P. 2012. "'A Stretch of Time': Extended Distribution and Narrative Accumulation in *Prison Break*." In *Time in Television Narrative: Exploring Temporality in Twenty-First-Century Programming*, edited by Melissa Ames, 43–55. Jackson: Univ. Press of Mississippi.

———. 2017. *Time, Technology and Narrative Form in Contemporary US Television Drama: Pause, Rewind, Record*. Cham, CH: Springer International Publishing.

Knisely, Lisa. 2008. "Between Black and White: The Ambiguous Politics of Race, Gender, and Desire in *Grey's Anatomy*." In *Grace Under Pressure: Grey's Anatomy Uncovered*, edited by Cynthia Burkhead and Hillary Robson, 121–28. Newcastle, UK: Cambridge Scholars Publishing.

Kozloff Sarah. 1988. *Invisible Storytellers: Voice-Over Narration in American Fiction Film*. Berkeley: Univ. of California Press.

Kristeva, Julia. 1980. *Desire in Language: A Semiotic Approach to Literature and Art*. Translated by Thomas Gora, Alice Jardine and Leon S. Roudiez. New York: Columbia Univ. Press. First published 1977.

———. 1981. "Women's Time." Translated by Alice Jardine Kristeva and Harry Blake. *Signs* 7, no. 1 (Autumn): 13–35.

———. 1984. *Revolution in Poetic Language*. Translated by Margaret Waller. New York: Columbia Univ. Press. First published 1974.

Kuhn, Annette. 1984. "Women's Genres." *Screen* 25 (1): 18–29.

Laist, Randy. 2011. *Looking for "Lost": Critical Essays on the Enigmatic Series*. Jefferson, NC: McFarland & Co.

LaRocque, Emma. 2010. *When the Other Is Me: Native Resistance Discourse 1850–1990*. Winnipeg: Univ. of Manitoba Press.

Lee, Michael J., and Leigh Moscowitz. 2013. "The Rich Bitch: Class and Gender on *The Real Housewives of NYC*." *Feminist Media Studies* 13 (1): 64–82.

Levin, Ira. 1972. *Stepford Wives*. New York: Random House.

Levine, Elana. 2008. "Distinguishing Television: The Changing Meanings of Television Liveness." *Media, Culture & Society* 30 (3): 393–409.

———. 2013. "*Grey's Anatomy*: Feminism." In *How to Watch Television*, edited by Ethan Thompson and Jason Mittell, 139–47. New York: New York Univ. Press.

Levine, Elana, and Michael Newman. 2012. *Legitimating Television: Media Convergence and Cultural Status.* London: Routledge.

Lévi-Strauss, Claude. 1976. "The Structural Study of Myth." In *Structural Anthropology,* translated by Claire Jacobson and Brooke Grundfest Schoepf, 206–31. New York: Basic Books.

Liberman, Rachael. 2015. "Hate-Watching the Housewives: Gender, Power, and the Pleasure of Judgement." In *The Fantasy of Reality: Critical Essays on the Real Housewives,* edited by Rachel E. Silverman, 109–21. New York: Peter Lang.

Lieber, Emma. 2013. "Realism's Housewives." *New England Review* 33 (4): 113–30.

Lopate, Carol. 1977. "Daytime Television: You'll Never Want to Leave Home." *Radical America* 11: 33–51.

Lotz, Amanda D. 2006. *Redesigning Women: Television after the Network Era.* Urbana: Univ. of Illinois Press.

———. 2007. *The Television Will Be Revolutionized.* New York: New York Univ. Press.

Luckett, Moya. 2014. "Playmates and Polygamists: Feminine Textuality in *Big Love, Sister Wives* and *The Girls Next Door.*" *Feminist Media Studies* 14 (4): 562–77.

Macdonald, Myra. 1995. *Representing Women: Myths of Femininity in the Popular Media.* New York: St. Martin's Press.

MacDowell, James. 2013. *Happy Endings in Hollywood Cinema: Cliché, Convention and the Final Couple.* Edinburgh: Edinburgh Univ. Press.

MacLeod, Erin. 2005. "Desperately Seeking Brenda: Writing the Self in *Six Feet Under.*" In *Reading "Six Feet Under": TV to Die For,* edited by Kim Akass and Janet McCabe, 135–45. London: I. B. Tauris.

Magill, David. 2011. "The *Lost* Boys and Masculinity Found." In *Looking for "Lost": Critical Essays on the Enigmatic Series,* edited by Randy Laist, 137–53. Jefferson, NC: McFarland.

Marby, A. Rochelle. 2006. "About a Girl: Female Subjectivity and Sexuality in Contemporary 'Chick' Culture." In *Chick Lit: The New Woman's Fiction,* edited by Suzanne Ferriss and Mallory Young, 191–206. New York: Routledge.

Martin, Brett. 2013. *Difficult Men: Behind the Scene of a Creative Revolution: From "The Sopranos" and "The Wire" to "Mad Men," and "Breaking Bad."* New York: Penguin.

Mattelart, Michele. 1981. "Women and the Cultural Industries." *Media Culture and Society* 4 (4): 133–51.

McCabe, Janet. 2005. "'Like, whatever': Claire, Female Identity and Growing Up Dysfunctional." In *Reading "Six Feet Under": TV to Die For*, edited by Kim Akass and Janet McCabe, 121–34. London: I. B. Tauris.

———. 2006. "What Is It with That Hair? Bree Van de Kamp and Policing Contemporary Femininity." In *Reading "Desperate Housewives": Beyond the White Picket Fence*, edited by Janet McCabe and Kim Akass, 74–85. London: I. B. Tauris.

McCabe, Janet, and Kim Akass, eds. 2006. *Reading "Desperate Housewives": Beyond the White Picket Fence*. London: I. B. Tauris.

———. 2007. *Quality TV: Contemporary American Television and Beyond*. London: Bloomsbury Publishing.

McDuffie, Kristi. 2012. "The Discourse of *Medium*: Time as a Narrative Device." In *Time in Television Narrative: Exploring Temporality in Twenty-First-Century Programming*, edited by Melissa Ames, 190–201. Jackson: Univ. Press of Mississippi.

McNutt, Myles. 2009. "Series Premiere: Nurse Jackie—'Pilot.'" *Cultural Learnings* (cultural-learnings.com). June 8, 2009.

Mellencamp, Patricia. 1986. "Situation Comedy, Feminism, and Freud: Discourses of Gracie and Lucy." In *Studies in Entertainment: Critical Approaches to Mass Culture*, edited by Tania Modleski, 80–95. Bloomington: Indiana Univ. Press.

Menon, Vinay. 2008. "Rise of the Anti-Heroines; Finally, Female Stars of TV Series are just as Loathsome and Messed Up as Male Counterparts." *Toronto Star*, March 10, 2008. http://www.thestar.com/opinion/columnists/2008/03/10/rise_of_tvs_antiheroines.html.

Mittell, Jason. 2006. "Narrative Complexity in Contemporary American Television." *The Velvet Light Trap* 58 (1): 29–40.

———. 2007. "Soap Operas and Primetime Seriality." *JustTV*. July 29, 2007. https://justtv.wordpress.com/2007/07/29/soap-operas-and-primetime-seriality/.

———. 2013. "Serial Orientations: Paratexts and Contemporary Complex Television." In *(Dis)Orienting Media and Narrative Mazes*, edited by Julia Eckel, Bernd Leiendecker, Daniela Olek, Christine Piepiorka, 165–82. Bielefeld: Transcript Verlag.

———. 2015a. *Complex TV: The Poetics of Contemporary Television Storytelling*. New York: New York Univ. Press.

———. 2015b. "AnTENNA, UnREAL: Anti-Heroes, Genre and Legitimation." *Antenna*, August 17, 2015. http://blog.commarts.wisc.edu/2015/08/17/antenna-unreal-anti-heroes-genreand-legitimation.

Modleski, Tania. 1979. "The Search for Tomorrow in Today's Soap Operas." *Film Quarterly* 33 (1): 12–21.

———. 2002. "Time and Desire in the Woman's Film." *Home Is Where the Heart Is: Studies in Melodrama and the Woman's Film*, edited by Christine Gledhill, 326–38. London: BFI Publishing. First published 1984.

———. 2007. *Loving with a Vengeance: Mass Produced Fantasies for Women*. London: Routledge. First published 1982.

Molina Guzmán, Isabel, and Angharad N. Valdivia. 2004. "Brain, Brow, and Booty: Latina Iconicity in U.S. Popular Culture." *Communication Review* 7: 205–21.

Mousoutzanis, Aris. 2012. "Temporality and Trauma in American Sci-Fi Television." In *Time in Television Narrative: Exploring Temporality in Twenty-First-Century Programming*, edited by Melissa Ames, 97–109. Jackson: Univ. Press of Mississippi.

Mroz, Matilda. 2012. *Temporality and Film Analysis*. Edinburgh: Edinburgh Univ. Press.

Mulvey, Laura. 1999. "Visual Pleasure and Narrative Cinema." In *Film Theory and Criticism: Introductory Readings*, edited by Leo Braudy and Marshall Cohen, 833–44. Oxford: Oxford Univ. Press. First published 1975.

Murray, Noel. 2008. "TV's Antihero Era Enters Its Second Decade." *AVclub.com*. June 9, 2008. http://www.avclub.com/article/tvs-antihero-era-enters-its-second-decade-28971.

Murray, Susan, and Laurie Ouellette. 2009. *Reality TV: Remaking Television Culture*. New York: New York Univ. Press.

Musial, Jennifer. 2014. "From 'Madonna' to 'Whore': Sexuality, Pregnancy, and Popular Culture." *Sexualities* 17 (4): 394–411.

Ndalianis Angela. 2005. "Television and the Neo-Baroque." In *The Contemporary Television Serial*, edited by Lucy Mazdon and Michael Hammond, 83–101. Edinburgh: Univ. of Edinburgh Press.

Negra, Diane. 2009a. "Time Crisis and the New Postfeminist Heterosexual Economy." In *Hetero: Queering Representations of Straightness*, edited by Sean Griffin, 173–90. Albany: State Univ. of New York Press.

———. 2009b. *What a Girl Wants? Fantasizing the Reclamation of Self in Postfeminism*. New York: Routledge.

Nochimson, Martha P. 2000. "Ally McBeal: Brightness Falls from the Air." *Film Quarterly* 53 (3): 25–32.

Nussbaum, Emily. 2013a. "Difficult Women: How 'Sex and the City' Lost Its Good Name." *The New Yorker*. July 29, 2013. http://www.newyorker.com/arts/critics/television/2013/07/29/130729crte_television_nussbaum?currentPage=all.

———. 2013b. "From *I Love Lucy* to *Breaking Bad*: How Ambitious Modern Television Rebelled Against Formula by Exploding It." *The Jepson Leadership Forum*. YouTube video by Richmond University. https://www.youtube.com/watch?v=3CdBN0en3RE.

———. 2018. "*Jane the Virgin* Is Not a Guilty Pleasure." *The New Yorker*. March 12, 2018. https://www.newyorker.com/magazine/2018/03/12/jane-the-virgin-is-not-a-guilty-pleasure.

Nygaard, Taylor, and Jorie Lagerwey. 2020. *Horrible White People: Gender, Genre, and Television's Precarious Whiteness*. New York: New York Univ. Press.

Panos, Maggie. 2012. "HBO Renews *Girls* and *Veep*." *Popsugar.com*. April 30, 2012. https://www.popsugar.com/entertainment/HBO-Girls-Renewed-Season-2-22898501.

Pape, Toni. 2012. "Temporalities on Collision Course: Time, Knowledge, and Temporal Critique in *Damages*." In *Time in Television Narrative: Exploring Temporality in Twenty-First-Century Programming*, edited by Melissa Ames, 165–77. Jackson: Univ. Press of Mississippi.

Petridis, Sotiris. 2017. "'I need an antiheroine': Female Antiheroes in American Quality Television." In *Hero or Villain? Essays on Dark Protagonists of Television*, edited by Abigail G. Scheg and Tamara Girardi, 74–83. Jefferson, NC: McFarland & Company.

Pinedo, Isabel C. 2021. *Difficult Women on Television Drama: The Gender Politics of Complex Women in Serial Narratives*. London: Routledge.

Poniewozik, James Keegan, and Rebecca Winters. 2007. "Antiheroine Chic." *Time* 170 (6): 57–59, August 6, 2007.

Powell, Anna. 2007. *Deleuze, Altered States and Film.* Edinburgh: Edinburgh Univ. Press.

Rakow, Lana F. 1986. "Feminist Approaches to Popular Culture: Giving Patriarchy Its Due." *Feminist Critiques of Popular Culture: A Special Issue of the Journal Communication* 9 (1): 19–42.

Rich, B. Ruby. 1998. *Chick Flicks: Theories and Memories of the Feminist Film Movement.* Durham, NC: Duke Univ. Press.

Ricoeur, Paul. 1990. *Time and Narrative.* Chicago: Univ. of Chicago Press. First published 1983.

Rogers, Steve. 2006. "Bravo's 'The Real Housewives of Orange County' to premiere March 21." *RealityTVworld.com.* January 6, 2006. http://www.realitytvworld.com/index/print.php?sid=3897.

Rose-Holt, Sundi. 2015. "Antiheroines are the New Antiheroes: The Killer Women of 'Penny Dreadful,' 'Orphan Black' and More." *IndieWire.com.* June 3, 2015. http://www.indiewire.com/2015/06/antiheroines-are-the-new-antiheroes-the-killer-women-of-penny-dreadful-orphan-black-and-more-61307/.

Rosenberg, Alyssa, and Emily Nussbaum. 2013. "Critic Proof." *Bloggin heads.tv.* Video, July 27, 2013. http://bloggingheads.tv/videos/20495.

Rowe, Kathleen K. "Roseanne: Unruly Woman as Domestic Goddess." 1997. In *Feminist Television Criticism: A Reader,* edited by Charlotte Brunsdon, Julie D'Acci, and Lynn Spiegel, 74–83. Oxford: Clarendon Press.

Ruddick, Sarah. 1990. *Maternal Thinking: Towards a Politics of Peace.* London: Women's Press.

Rustad, Gry C., and Timotheus Vermeulen. 2012. "'Did You Get Pears?': Temporality and Temps Mortality in *The Wire, Mad Men,* and *Arrested Development.*" In *Time in Television Narrative: Exploring Temporality in Twenty-First-Century Programming,* edited by Melissa Ames, 153–64. Jackson: Univ. Press of Mississippi.

Seel, Tara Lynne. 2006. "'Hastening Together to Perfect Felicity': The Antiheroine's Negotiation of Identity and Discovery of Agency in the Feminist Gothic." Master's Thesis, Univ. of Regina.

Shadraconis, Sophon. 2013. "Leaders and Heroes: Modern Day Archetypes." *LUX: A Journal of Transdisciplinary Writing and Research from Claremont Graduate University* 3 (1): 1–13.

Sharp, Sharon. "Disciplining the Housewife in *Desperate Housewives* and Domestic Reality Television." In *Reading "Desperate Housewives":*

Beyond the White Picket Fence, edited by Janet McCabe and Kim Akass, 119–28. London: I. B. Tauris.

Sharrock, Alison. 2018. "How Do We Read a (W)hole?: Dubious First Thoughts about the Cognitive Turn." In *Intratextuality and Latin Literature*, edited by Stephen Harrison, Stavros Frangoulidis, and Theodore D. Papanghelis, 15–31. Berlin: De Gruyter.

Shimpach, Shawn. 2010. *Television in Transition: The Life and Afterlife of the Narrative Action Hero*. Chichester: Wiley-Blackwell.

Showalter, Elaine. 1977. *A Literature of Their Own: British Women Novelists from Brontë to Lessing*. Princeton, NJ: Princeton Univ. Press.

Silverman, Gillian, and Sarah Hagelin. 2018. "Shame TV: Feminist Antiaspirationalism in HBO's Girls." *Signs: Journal of Women in Culture and Society* 43 (4): 877–904.

Silverman, Rachel E., ed. 2015. *The Fantasy of Reality: Critical Essays on the Real Housewives*. New York: Peter Lang.

Smith, Greg M. 2007. *Beautiful TV: The Art and Argument of Ally McBeal*. Austin: Univ. of Texas Press.

Smith, Murray. 1995. *Engaging Characters: Fiction, Emotion, and the Cinema*. Oxford: Clarendon Press.

Spangler, Lynn C. 2003. *Television Women from Lucy to Friends: Fifty Years of Sitcoms and Feminism*. Westport, CT: Praeger Publishers.

Spigel, Lynn. 1992. *Make Room for TV: Television and the Family Ideal in Postwar America*. Chicago: Univ. of Chicago Press.

———. 2004. "Theorizing the Bachelorette: 'Waves' of Feminist Media Studies." *Signs: Journal of Women in Culture and Society* 30 (1): 1209–21.

Spinelli, Frank. 2014. "Reality Stars Perpetuate Negative Italian Stereotypes." *Huffpost*, May 4, 2014. https://www.huffpost.com/entry/reality-stars-real-housewives_b_4899681.

Squires, Lauren. 2014. "Class and Productive Avoidance in *The Real Housewives* Reunions." *Discourse, Context and Media* 6: 33–44.

Stanley, Alessandra. "Wrought in Rhimes's Image." *New York Times*, September 18, 2014. https://www.nytimes.com/2014/09/21/arts/television/viola-davis-plays-shonda-rhimess-latest-tough-heroine.html.

Streamas, John. 2010. "Closure And 'Colored People's Time.'" In *Time: Limits and Constraints*, edited by Jo Alyson Parker, Paul André Harris, and Christian Steineck, 219–39. Leiden: Brill.

Swanson, Gillian. 1981. "Dallas: Part II." *Framework* 15/16/17: 81–85.

Tally, Margaret. 2016. *The Rise of the Anti-Heroine in TV's Third Golden Age*. Cambridge: Cambridge Scholars Publishing.

Tully, Meg. 2020. "Watching a Trainwreck Feminism." *Women's Studies in Communication*. https://doi.org/10.1080/07491409.2020.1831868.

Turim, Maureen. 1989. *Flashbacks in Film: Memory and History*. New York: Routledge.

Turow, Joseph. 2010. *Playing Doctor: Television, Storytelling, and Medical Power*. Ann Arbor: Univ. of Michigan Press.

Walker, Rebecca, ed. 1995. *To Be Real: Telling the Truth and Changing the Face of Feminism*. New York: Doubleday.

Warner, Kristen J. 2014. "The Racial Logic of Grey's Anatomy: Shonda Rhimes and Her 'Post-Civil Rights, Post-Feminist' Series." *Television & New Media* 16 (7): 631–47.

———. 2015. "They Gon' Think You Loud Regardless: Ratchetness, Reality Television, and Black Womanhood." *Camera Obscura* 30, no. 1 (88): 129–53.

West, Carolyn M. 2012. "Mammy, Jezebel, Sapphire, and Their Homegirls: Developing an 'Oppositional Gaze' toward the Images of Black Women." In *Lectures on the Psychology of Women*, edited Joan Chrisler, Carla Golden, and Patricia Rozee, 286–99. New York: McGraw Hill.

West-Pavlov, Russell. 2013. *Temporalities*. New York: Routledge.

Wilhelm, Julie. 2013. "Money Can't Buy Them Class Security: The Stories of the *Real Housewives* of Bravo TV." *Storytelling: A Critical Journal of Pop Narrative* 13 (1): 32–48.

Williams, Linda. 1998. "Melodrama Revised." In *Refiguring American Film Genres: History and Theory*, edited by Nick Browne, 42–88. Berkeley: Univ. of California Press.

Williams, Raymond. 1974. *Television: Technology and Cultural Form*. London: Fontana.

Wolf, Naomi. 1991. *The Beauty Myth: How Images of Beauty Are Used against Women*. London: Vintage.

———. 1998. *Promiscuities: The Secret Struggle for Womanhood*. New York: Fawcett Books.

Wolfe, Susan J., and Lee Ann Roripaugh. 2006. "The (In)visible Lesbian: Anxieties of Representation in The L Word." In *Reading The L Word: Outing Contemporary Television*, edited by Kim Akass and Janet McCabe. London: I. B. Tauris.

Woolf, Virginia. 2000. *A Room of One's Own*. London: Penguin Books. First published 1929.

Zanger, Anat. 2006. *Film Remakes as Ritual Disguise: From Carmen to Ripley*. Amsterdam: Amsterdam Univ. Press.

Index

1950s television, 7, 17, 18n7, 58, 130, 153
1960s television, 18, 139–40
1970s television, 18–19, 27, 127, 139–40
1980s television, 19, 22, 80
1990s television, 19–20, 111
24 (2001–10), 8, 26

abortion, 18, 127
Adventures of Ozzie and Harriet, The (1952–66), 17, 153
Ally McBeal (1997–2002), 19, 20, 27, 40, 111
Anna Karenina (novel 1878), 116, 125
antihero, 1–2, 7–11, 16–17, 141
Austen, Jane, 139n21

Bachelor, The (2002–), 87n6
Barthes, Roland, 73
Being Mary Jane (2013–19), 42–46, 119–23
Better Things (2016–), 21, 114n7
Big Love (2006–11), 138
Bravo wink, 48, 92
Breaking Bad (2008–13), 1, 9, 11
broadcast vs. cable, 114. *See also* HBO

Buffy the Vampire Slayer (1997–2003), 14n13, 19
Butler, Judith, 24, 93, 93n11, 109, 109n3

Cagney & Lacey (1981–88), 5n3
cardinal functions, 73–74
Cashmere Mafia (2008), 4n1, 137–38
Chicago Hope (1994–2000), 52
chick flicks, 2–3, 147–48. *See also* woman's film
chick lit, 2–3, 147–48
chrononormativity, 24–25, 31–44, 50–51, 63–78, 104–15
Cixous, Hélène, 57
cliffhanger, 80, 105–6
complex TV, 1–6, 22–28, 87–88
confessional (reality TV), 46–48, 61, 100–101
CSI (2000–2015), 87, 92n10

Dallas (1978–91), 18, 22, 140
Damages (2007–12), 5, 26n24
Daria (1997–2001), 14n13
Days and Nights of Molly Dodd, The (1987–91), 27, 40
death, 33–37, 68–70, 125n15

175

Defenders, The (2017), 87
Deleuze, Gilles, 25, 61, 109, 141–42; Deleuze and Guattari, 35n4, 107n1
Designing Women (1986–93), 19, 137
Desperate Housewives (2004–12), 72–74, 79, 113–19, 121–22, 129–36, 139–40
Dexter (2006–13), 1, 8
dialogism. *See* intertextuality
Diary of a Mad Housewife (film 1970), 140n22

Eco, Umberto, 109
ellipsis (textual temporality), 71–73
episodicity, 22, 80, 105, 145
ER (1994–2009), 52, 141

Faludi, Susan, 19, 110, 140n22
Fatal Attraction (film 1987), 120, 125
Father Knows Best (1954–60), 153
Feminine Mystique, The, 116n10, 130
Feuer, Jane, 46
Fiske, John, 3, 5n3, 25
flashback, 22–23, 53–62, 77–78
flashforward, 22–23, 62–74, 77–80
FlashForward (2009–10), 26, 73
flash-sideways, 74–78
Flip or Flop (2013), 87n6
Friedan, Betty. *See Feminine Mystique, The*

Game, The (2006–15), 43n9
George Burns and Gracie Allen Show, The (1950–58), 17, 130, 132
Gilmore Girls (2000–2007), 111

Girlfriends (2000–2008), 43n9, 139
Girls (2012–17), 32–37, 53, 70–71, 104–6, 114, 128, 138–39
Girls Next Door, The (2005–10), 138
Golden Girls (1985–92), 120, 125, 127
Good Times (1974–79), 18
Grey's Anatomy (2005–), 6, 50–62, 63–70, 74–78, 119–23, 134, 148

Halberstam, J., 12n8, 14, 24–25, 31, 38, 51–52, 114
Handmaid's Tale, The (2017–), 5, 62n9
happy ending, 67, 71–72, 89–91, 96n13, 103–5
HBO, 8, 33, 114
hegemonic order, 2, 11, 24–25, 63, 97, 109–12, 147. *See also* sociosymbolic order
hegemony. *See* hegemonic order; sociosymbolic order
housewife, 95, 129–36
How I Met Your Mother (2005–14), 26, 31
How to Get Away with Murder (2014–20), 5, 140

I Love Lucy (1951–57), 17, 18n17
Insecure (2016–), 21, 139
intratextuality, 79–81, 106–7

Jane the Virgin (2014–19), 5, 26–27
Jeffersons, The (1975–85), 18
Jezebel stereotype, 122–23
Judging Amy (1999–2005), 19, 111
Julia (1968–71), 139

Kristeva, Julia, 11, 13, 24, 38, 63, 73, 108–9

lady, 14, 96n12, 99–102
Law and Order (1999–), 87
Leave It to Beaver (1957–63), 17
Lévi-Strauss, Claude, 109
Lipstick Jungle (2008–9), 4n1, 137
liveness, 42–46, 52n3, 107
Looking for Mr. Goodbar (film 1977), 125
Lost (2004–10), 26, 49, 73
L Word, The (2004–9), 127n16

Madame Bovary (novel 1856), 125
Mad Men (2007–15), 1, 9, 49, 141
Madonna/whore dichotomy, 13, 42, 58, 117, 122
Mary Tyler Moore Show, The (1970–77), 18, 43, 46, 127, 138
masculinity, 1–2, 5n3, 9–10, 16–17, 26–27, 49, 63
masquerade, 112
matrixial seriality, 82–103
Maude (1972–78), 18, 127
medical drama, 6, 52
Medium (2005–11), 26n24
melodrama, 4, 73, 147. See also woman's film
Mental (2009), 52
Mildred Pierce (novel 1941; film 1945), 131
Million Dollar Listing (2006–), 87n6
minor literature, 35n4
miscarriage, 42, 125–27
Mittell, Jason, 2, 6–9, 11, 17, 22, 80

Modleski, Tania, 4, 18, 27, 80, 88
motherhood, 10–13, 42–44, 60, 64, 71, 75, 96–98, 135
Mrs. Fletcher (2019), 114n7
Mulvey, Laura, 13–14, 116
Murphy Brown (1988–98), 7, 19, 46
My So-Called Life (1994–95), 19, 40

narrative complexity. See complex TV
Nurse Jackie (2009–15), 37–40, 52, 79–80, 139–41
Nurses, The (1962–65), 139
Nussbaum, Emily, 3, 11, 16–17, 20, 26–27, 120

open memory, 57
Orange Is the New Black (2013–19), 5, 53n4, 108, 140
Orphan Black (2013–17), 5

Peyton Place (1964–69), 140
polygamy, 47, 132–33, 138
postmodernism, 40
post-network, 108
Providence (1999–2002), 111

queer time, 25. See also Halberstam

Real Housewives of Atlanta, The (2008–), 83–86, 91–97, 99–101
Real Housewives of Beverly Hills, The (2010–), 85–87, 93–96, 100–103
Real Housewives of Dallas, The (2016–), 83, 86n5

Real Housewives of DC, The (2010), 83, 86n5
Real Housewives of Miami, The (2011–13), 83, 86n5, 87n6
Real Housewives of New Jersey, The (2009–), 48, 83, 85, 86n5, 88, 96n13
Real Housewives of New York City, The (2008–), 83, 85, 88–91
Real Housewives of Orange County, The (2006–), 82–91, 96–98, 103, 139
Real Housewives of Potomac, The (2016–), 83, 86n5
Real Housewives of Salt Lake City, The (2020–), 83, 86n5
Real World, The (1992–), 20, 87n6
repetition, 24, 55n7, 65n10, 79n1, 107–11, 115–42
respectability, 44n10, 96n12
reunion episode, 61–62, 86, 89, 96–98
rhizome, 107n1
Rhoda (1974–78), 18
rich bitch, 82
romantic comedy, 26
Roseanne (1988–97), 19, 112n5

Sapphire stereotype, 58–60
Scandal (2012–18), 5
Scarlet Letter, The (novel 1850), 124
season finale, 45, 68–72, 79–80, 89–91, 103–5
second wave feminism, 18–19, 127, 130, 139–40
Sex and the City (1998–2004), 16–20, 27, 43, 111, 120, 125–27, 137–38
sex/sexuality, 12–16, 42, 52, 113–29, 147–48

Sister Wives (2010–), 47, 132–33, 135–36, 138
Six Feet Under (2001–5), 6, 40–42, 68–71, 123–28, 134–36
Smilf (2017–19), 114n7
soap operas, and "soapy," 3–6, 16–18, 27, 50, 80–81, 88, 105, 147–48
social surrealism, 40
sociosymbolic order, 11, 13, 145. *See also* hegemonic order
Sopranos, The (1999–2007), 1, 7–9, 115, 141
Spigel, Lynn, 4, 46–148
St. Elsewhere (1982–88), 22, 52, 141
Stepford Wives (novel 1972; film 1975), 130–31
Supernatural (2005–20), 26, 31, 49
Survivor franchise, 87n6

temporal turn, 23
"time of history," 24–25, 38, 63, 73
Transparent (2014–19), 5, 113, 148
Turim, Maureen, 25, 53, 55, 57–58

UnREAL (2015–18), 11
unruly woman, 112n5, 137

villain/villainess, 9, 18, 75–76, 116–23, 128
voice-over, 37–39, 48, 54–56, 64–65, 74

wedding, 89–91, 100, 103–5, 126–27
Westworld (2016–), 5, 62n9
Why Women Kill (2019–), 21

Williams, Linda, 73
Williams, Raymond, 32n2
woman's film, 27, 147–48. *See also* melodrama

woman's novel, 4, 27, 147–48
Woman Under the Influence, A (1974), 140n22
Woolf, Virginia, 4, 27, 37

Yael Levy is a television scholar and a teaching fellow at the Tisch School of Film and Television at Tel Aviv University. Her articles on gender, race, sexuality, and textuality in television have appeared in *Feminist Media Studies, Continuum: Journal of Media & Cultural Studies*, and Lexington Books. Her coedited anthology (with Miri Talmon) *Israeli Television: Local Visions, Global Contexts* was published by Routledge in 2020.